$24.50

D0521198

PROFESSIONAL
Kitchen
Design ◆ ◆ ◆ ◆

By Murray Shaw

Craftsman Book Company
6058 Corte del Cedro / P.O. Box 6500
Carlsbad, CA 92018

Looking for other construction reference manuals?

Craftsman has the books to fill your needs.
Call toll-free 1-800-829-8123 or write to
Craftsman Book Company, P.O. Box 6500, Carlsbad, CA 92018
for a FREE CATALOG of books, videos, audios
and computer software.

Library of Congress Cataloging-in-Publication Data

Shaw, Murray.
  Professional kitchen design / Murray Shaw.
    p.   cm.
  Includes index.
  ISBN 1-57218-014-5
  1. Kitchens--Design.   I. Title.
TX653.S525   1995   95-195181
643'.3--dc20   CIP

©1995 Craftsman Book Company

Photos courtesy of Aristocraft, Inc.
P.O. Box 420
Jasper, IN 47547

Illustrations by Mike Leffert

Contents

CHAPTER 1
Kitchen Design Basics

When it comes to our homes, more is usually better than less. More space is better than less space. More bathrooms, more bedrooms, more lighting, more glass area, more decorative treatments, a more varied floor plan, more appliances and built-ins are all better than less. Of course, more of what makes a home desirable doesn't come cheap. The extra convenience and satisfaction costs more. Usually lots more.

And that's too bad. Because most of us in the construction industry don't have clients with unlimited resources. The people we build for have only so much money to spend. The homes we build and the kitchens we remodel can have only so much of what we consider desirable. The choices we make are usually compromises between what's possible and what's practical. If that's the kind of work you handle (or expect to handle), this book is full of good ideas for you and your clients. Here's why.

In the kitchen business, the limited resources don't prevent you from doing a good job. It's possible to design and build a budget kitchen that's every bit as functional, convenient, attractive and comfortable as a kitchen that costs several times as much. You just have to master the basics of good kitchen design. And that's the purpose of this book: to teach a very specialized skill – contemporary kitchen design.

Between the covers of this book I'll share with you what I've learned from a half century in the kitchen business. You'll discover very quickly that there's more to kitchen design than just grouping all the right appliances within easy reach. You'll learn to associate certain appliances with certain types of work area. You'll learn to plan for traffic flow, lighting, ventilation, comfort, view and aesthetics. You'll discover here a wealth of practical information and novel ideas you won't find in kitchen design books or the monthly homeowner magazines.

The Modern Kitchen

Today's kitchen is a far cry from those of years past when we washed dishes by hand and heated the water to do it on a wood- or coal-burning stove. Not many of today's homemakers remember the old-fashioned icebox and the mess it made when the drip pan overflowed. Modern appliances have changed the way we use

our kitchens. Most of the tedious work is now done for us automatically, leaving us time for other work or entertainment.

Built-in conventional, convection and microwave ovens, range tops, ranges and refrigerators have changed the appearance of the modern kitchen. You can recess small appliances into the walls or store them in appliance "garages," leaving counters free and uncluttered. Other appliances make waste disposal quick and nearly effortless.

But a kitchen loaded with appliances and labor-saving conveniences isn't necessarily a functional, convenient kitchen. I wrote this book to show you how to integrate kitchen equipment and furnishings into a practical, comfortable and beautiful part of any home.

It will be of particular interest to:

♦ *Kitchen remodelers* – Redesigning an inefficient, awkward kitchen into a model of modern convenience is probably the best test of any kitchen designer's skill. Doing it with the existing floor plan, on a budget and without evicting the owners from their home while construction is going on almost takes a magician. That's the type of magic I intend to teach.

♦ *Builders* – A well-planned kitchen can sell a house better than any other room. People are aware today of what is or isn't a functional kitchen. The first thing buyers look for is the location of the major appliances, and whether their positions make sense. Builders should be able to evaluate an architect's preliminary design and recommend changes when necessary.

♦ *Kitchen materials salespeople* – This book will help you and your staff advise clients about their kitchen equipment needs and layout.

♦ *Teachers in architectural schools and colleges* – You can supplement classroom training with practical, direct involvement with the most common kitchen design problems.

♦ *Architects* – Every home designer needs specialized training in kitchen design – not only style and structure, but function and arrangement as well.

♦ *Interior designers* – Designing a functional kitchen goes far beyond selecting cabinets, countertop material, appliances, and lighting fixtures. Arranging the parts of a kitchen is even more important. A designer who specializes in remod-

eling also has to know something about the building trades that relate to kitchen design and construction. Can this wall be taken out? How far can the sink be moved from its drain stub? What effect will changing the kitchen have on the home's electrical and plumbing systems? I'll answer those questions here.

♦ *Homeowners* – You'll get better results if you understand the principles of kitchen design, and can talk the same language as the professionals you hire and rely on.

Now that I've explained where this book is headed, let's get started. We'll begin with some simple rules for kitchen counters: five rules you can follow on every kitchen job you have.

Begin With the Counters

Here are the five basic kitchen design rules for counters:

♦ *Rule 1:* Counters on both sides of the sink.

♦ *Rule 2:* Counters on both sides of the range top.

♦ *Rule 3:* Counter on at least one side of a wall oven.

♦ *Rule 4:* Counter opposite hinges of the refrigerator.

♦ *Rule 5:* Counter opposite hinges of a pantry door.

Basic Rule 1 - Counters by Sinks

Here's the most important of the five basic kitchen design rules: Always have ample counter space on both sides of the sink, even if it's in an island or peninsula. Allow at least 24 to 36 inches of space between the sink and a major cooking appliance. If the sink is next to the refrigerator or wall oven, provide at least 18 inches of countertop. An island sink requires a minimum of 24 inches of space on each side.

Most food preparation is done near the sink. Remember, the sink is also the primary clean-up area. Dirty dishes and utensils will usually accumulate beside the sink any time food is being prepared.

It's not practical to locate the sink at the end of a counter. Not only will it have counter space on just one side, but splashing and spill-overs become a nuisance, especially if water pressure is high.

A   Before: A poorly arranged stove and sink

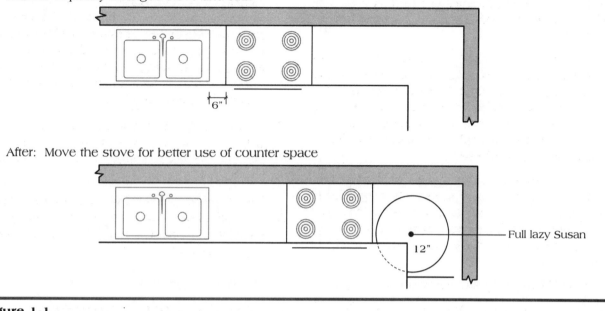

B   After: Move the stove for better use of counter space

— Full lazy Susan

Figure 1-1
Planning counter space by the sink

In Figure 1-1 A, the designer placed the range too close to the sink, leaving barely 6 inches of counter space between the two. That's not even enough space for a pot or pan. Think about using the sink while cooking. Who wants soapsuds in their scrambled eggs?

With so much available counter space at the right of the range, there seems to be no logical reason for the arrangement. Figure 1-1 B shows a much better location for the range. There's also another reason to move the range. If you install it a minimum of 12 inches from the internal corner, there's room for a full lazy Susan (revolving) cabinet under the sink. This puts an otherwise useless dead end corner to good use.

The layout in Figure 1-2 shows about 18 inches of counter between the sink and the wall oven.

Consider 18 inches the minimum for this situation. That's just enough room to set down a roasting pan when you take it from the oven. If the refrigerator was in that position instead of the wall oven, the space could be as little as 12 inches, but 18 inches would be better there too. Just be sure that in a situation like this one, the largest span of countertop is between the range or cooktop and the sink, because that's the main food preparation area.

Basic Rule 2 - Counters by Cooking Appliances

All ranges, whether they're freestanding, slip-in, drop-in, eye-level, or down-draft units, must have counters on both sides. Figure 1-3 A shows what happens if you don't follow that rule. Notice that the

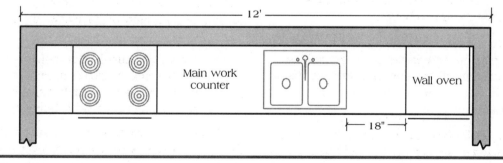

Main work counter

Wall oven

Figure 1-2
Leave at least 18 inches of countertop next to the wall oven

A   Before: Pot handles present a danger

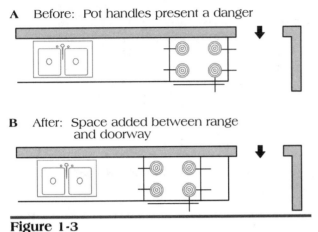

B   After: Space added between range and doorway

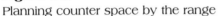

Figure 1-3
Planning counter space by the range

A   Before: Not enough work space

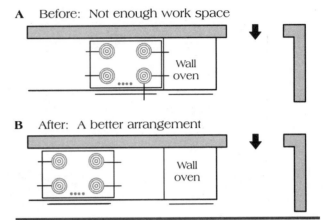

B   After: A better arrangement

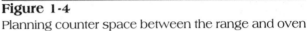

Figure 1-4
Planning counter space between the range and oven

range is at the end of the counter by the entrance to the kitchen. There are two mistakes here. First, this example breaks Rule 2; there's counter space on only one side of the range. That's a problem if you're cooking for a crowd. When you're using all four burners, you'll have to reach over a steaming pot to move something from an outside burner to the counter on the opposite side – a risky business.

There's another problem here, an even more serious one. If all four burners are in use, the pot handles nearest the doorway may stick out beyond the edge of the range top where they could be easily bumped, tipping the pan over. Figure 1-3 B shows a better arrangement. It's much more convenient. The danger from protruding handles is nearly eliminated if you install a cabinet between the entrance and the range, even if the cabinet is only 12 inches wide.

Don't place a cooktop directly next to a wall oven. Leave at least enough space so that the pot handles don't contact the oven cabinet as they do in Figure 1-4 A. And better yet, leave a space wide enough to hold a large baking or roasting pan. Figure 1-4 B is a much better layout.

Basic Rule 3 - Counter Next to the Wall Oven

A wall oven needs only one counter, and it's not important which side of the oven it's on. What is important is the location of the oven itself. Don't install it against a wall that defines the entrance to the kitchen, as in Figure 1-5 A. People can't get in and out of the kitchen when the oven door is open, such as when the cook is basting a roast or turkey.

Notice the room entrance in Figure 1-5 B. There's no problem getting around the oven door to enter or leave, even if someone is using the oven.

Basic Rule 4 - Counter by the Refrigerator

For convenience, the refrigerator door should swing away from adjacent counter space. That makes it easier to stock the refrigerator and keeps the electric bill down because the refrigerator door doesn't have to stay open so long. Be sure there's counter space on the side of the refrigerator opposite the hinges. Most

A   Oven door blocks entrance

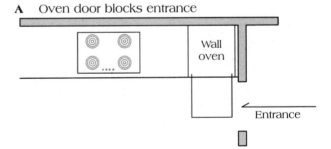

B   There's room to pass an open oven door

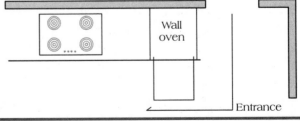

Figure 1-5
Planning counter space next to the oven

Figure 1-6
Planning counter placement for refrigerators

refrigerators come with hinges on the right side, but they are usually reversible.

Side-by-side refrigerators generally have the freezer section on the left side as you face it. Since you open the refrigerator section more frequently, it's more important to have counter space to the left. Figure 1-6 shows preferable counter locations for all three types of refrigerators.

Figure 1-7 A is a classic example of a poorly-located refrigerator. You either have to walk around the door, or cross to the other side of the kitchen to set things down. Figure 1-7 B is a much better arrangement and uses the same amount of wall space.

Avoid installing a refrigerator in a niche unless there's counter space nearby. In Figure 1-8 A you see a refrigerator that's recessed into a wall, with an island opposite. In that case, make sure the space between the refrigerator and the island is greater than the width of the door. For example, if the refrigerator is 36 inches wide, the space must be at least that. But 39 to 42 inches is better.

Also, be careful when you install a refrigerator with its side against any wall. Some refrigerators with deep storage in the doors or storage that extends all the way to the bottom of the door have to be opened more than 90 degrees to remove shelves or drawers inside the box. You can see the problem in Figure 1-8 B. The niche or side wall must not extend past the refrigerator's hinges.

If the refrigerator door opens into a doorway, be sure the doorway is wider than the refrigerator door. Note Figure 1-8 C.

A   Counter is behind the door

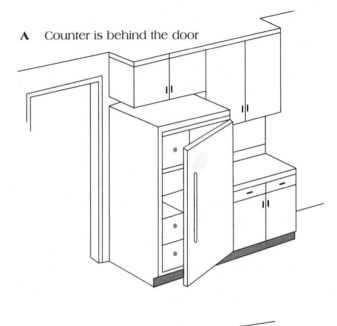

B   Better refrigerator placement

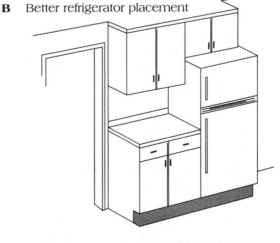

Figure 1-7
Make it convenient to use the refrigerator

A   Leave enough space in front of the refrigerator

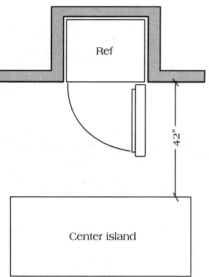

B   Don't prevent the refrigerator door from opening past 90 degrees

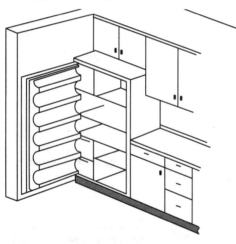

C   These doors swing clear

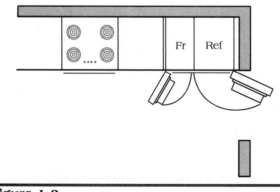

Figure 1-8
Allow space for the refrigerator door to open

Basic Rule 5 - Counter by the Pantry

If possible, find room for a pantry cabinet to store regularly-used non-perishable staple items in the kitchen itself. If you also have space for a pantry somewhere else such as the garage or utility room, use that one for storage of seldom-used items. No matter where you locate the pantry, nearby counter space is essential. The rules for placing the counter are the same as for the refrigerator – place the counter nearest the pantry door's opening. The user needs this space to sort, load and unload groceries.

If there's absolutely no room for traditional counter space, build it into the pantry itself. Install a pull-out shelf under a pantry shelf and 30 to 36 inches from the floor. The shelf that supports the pull-out shelf should be at least 15 inches deep. The other shelves can be only 12 inches deep.

Make sure the 15-inch shelf is well supported, either with metal L brackets or a wood support. Note Figure 1-9. Then attach sturdy slides to side cleats or the shelf support, and to the shelf. Or you can use roller bearing supports sold by most hardware stores and building supply dealers. Acuride makes a 14-inch track for this purpose. Graffamerica and Blum also manufacture slide units that feature an automatic stop to prevent the sliding shelf from pulling out all the way. Fasten the entire assembly to the supporting wall with toggle bolts or expansion fasteners.

The Kitchen Design Triangle

Kitchen designers think of the major work stations in a kitchen as being arranged at the points of a triangle when seen in plan view. The sink is the apex of the triangle. The range or cooktop is at the second point of the triangle and the refrigerator is at the third. Of course, not just any triangle will do. There are good triangles and bad triangles. The precise location of the range and refrigerator and their distance from the sink and each other determine how convenient the kitchen is.

The best size for the perimeter of the triangle is about 21 feet or less. Figure 1-10 shows a triangle where the distance from the sink to the range is 6 feet 5 inches, and from the sink to the refrigerator is just over 8 feet. The range and the refrigerator are also about 8 feet apart. This triangle is larger than the recommended maximum. But the extra step it takes to get from the refrigerator to the sink is offset by the convenience of the extra-long counter next to the refrigerator.

A Shelf with metal bracket

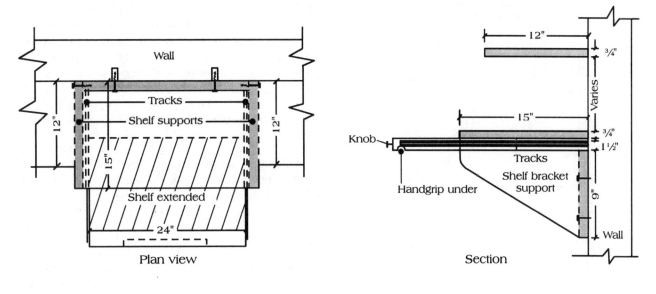

B Shelf with wood support

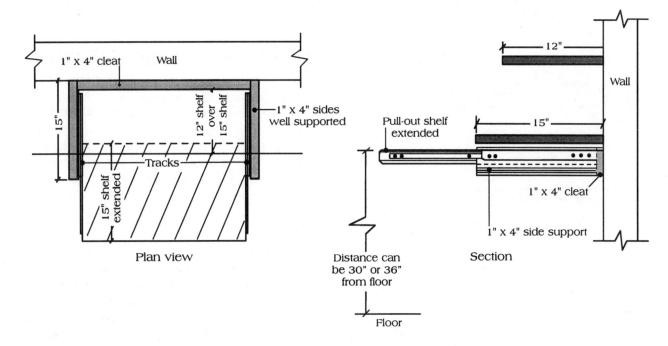

Figure 1-9
Pull-out shelf inside pantry cabinet

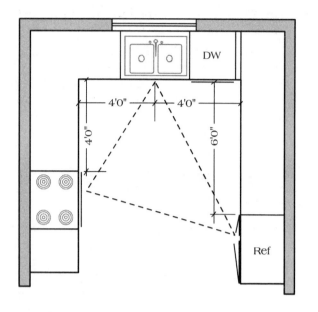

Figure 1-10
A well-proportioned work triangle

The triangle size is by no means inflexible. But it does give you a guide to follow. You don't want to design a kitchen where the user needs roller skates to move from one work area to another.

Figure 1-11 A looks OK at first glance. But study the drawing. Notice that the range and refrigerator are placed incorrectly. They disobey both Rules 2 and 4 for counters. There's counter space on just one side of the range top, and the side of the cooktop is in the entrance passageway. Also, the counter is on the wrong side of the refrigerator and the freezer door will hit the wall when it's fully open.

Now look at Figure 1-11 B. The triangle is the same size and shape, but this kitchen is functional. All the placement problems in Figure 1-11 A were solved by switching the positions of the range and refrigerator. The location of the range allows an 18-inch-wide base or drawer cabinet beside the range, and leaves counter space for both pairs of burners.

Notice when you switch appliances this way, you usually have to relocate the utility services. If there's not already an electrical outlet at the old range location, it's relatively easy to tap off a nearby existing outlet and run the wiring up to the ceiling, across, and down again between the studs. That provides power for the refrigerator.

Moving the range may be more of a problem. For an electric range, you might have to install a new circuit at the service box if there isn't already 220-volt service to the kitchen. For a gas range, you can probably run the line around the edge of the room behind the base cabinets. Or you can run it under the floor. In

A This triangle doesn't work

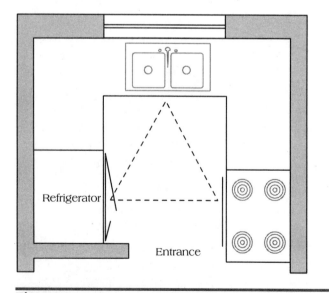

B Rearranging appliances solves the problem

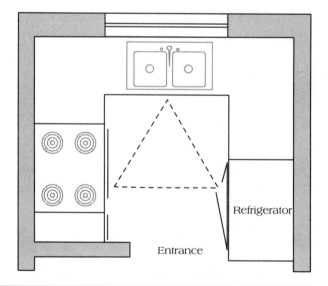

Figure 1-11
Consider both triangle size and appliance placement

A An inconvenient arrangement

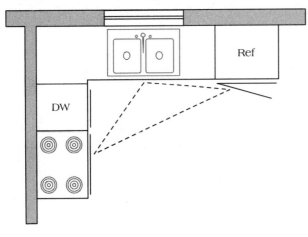

B This variation works better

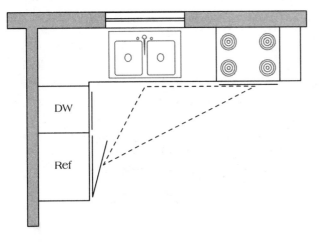

C This arrangement works best

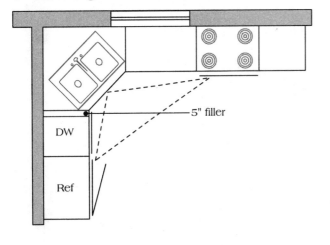

5" filler

Figure 1-12
Finding the best arrangement for an
L-shaped kitchen

either case, there must be an easily accessible shutoff valve so the range can be moved or serviced without cutting off gas service to the entire house.

In an L-shaped kitchen, two points of the triangle are often on the same wall. Note Figure 1-12 A. That's not the ideal solution and generally makes for an inconvenient kitchen layout. The range and refrigerator are both placed incorrectly and violate Rules 2 and 4 for counter space.

Figure 1-12 B shows a better way to arrange this kitchen. Now there's counter space on both sides of the range. Counter space over the dishwasher is handy to the refrigerator.

The arrangement in Figure 1-12 C is better yet. The sink is in what was a nearly useless corner in Figures 1-12 A and B. That creates more space for base cabinets. And the sink is still by the window. Notice that there's more counter space between the sink and the range. The 5-inch filler between the sink cabinet and the dishwasher allows enough standing room when the dishwasher door is open. Always use a filler in this situation. Never install the dishwasher flush with the angle to a corner sink.

Notice also that you can vent the range directly outdoors when you move it from an interior wall to an exterior wall.

The Triangle and a Center Island

A large kitchen with an island presents more of a challenge to the designer. You must place the range or cooktop and the refrigerator logically, but not too far apart. Be especially careful to avoid having the island intrude into the work triangle.

It's possible to place the main sink in the island if the island is large enough, but it's more common to put a smaller secondary sink there.

Note Figure 1-13 A. You'd have to walk around the island to get from the refrigerator to either the main sink or the cooktop, and there's no counter space next to the refrigerator. Both the wall oven and the refrigerator need adjacent counter space. But space beside the refrigerator is most important. In this arrangement, the small sink in the island is located at the end of the island. That violates Rule 1 which requires counter space on both sides of a sink.

There are two ways to solve this problem. In Figure 1-13 B the positions of the refrigerator and the wall oven are reversed so that each has counter space next to it. At one time it might have been foolish to place a refrigerator and an oven side by side. But

A Traffic is obstructed between main work areas

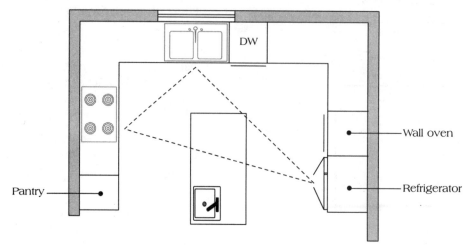

B Triangle isn't interrupted by the island

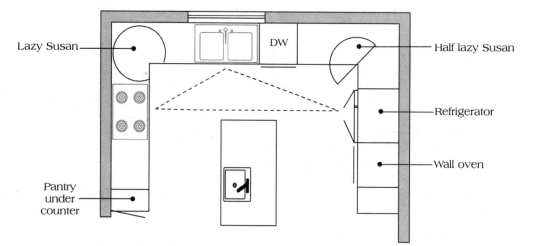

C Same space, better arrangement

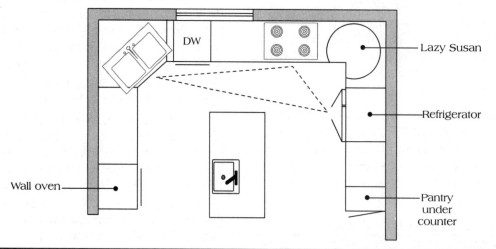

Figure 1-13
Make sure the island isn't in the traffic pattern

A Plan view

B Elevation

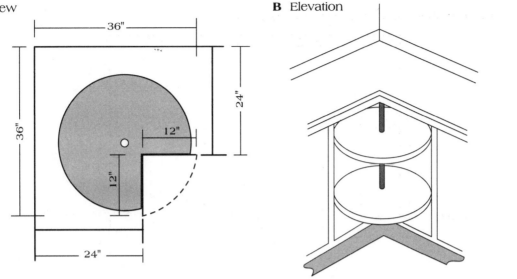

Figure 1-14
Full lazy Susan

modern ovens and refrigerators are exceptionally well insulated. Heat from the oven won't affect the refrigerator. Anyhow, the space between the oven and the surrounding cabinet offers extra insulation.

The lazy Susan cabinet makes good use of the dead corner in the base cabinet. Notice that we've moved the small sink away from the edge of the island. Now the island doesn't get in the way of the triangle. Here we haven't included the wall oven in the triangle. That's acceptable kitchen design. But be sure there's at least 15 inches of counter space adjacent to the wall oven.

It's possible to place the range top in the island. For an electric range, simply run the wiring under the floor or through a channel in the slab. A gas range presents some extra requirements. Most codes today require the plumbing to be enclosed in the floor, and the shutoff valve must be easily accessible in the cabinet beneath the range top.

The exhaust fan over an island range must have a higher drawing capacity than one next to a wall because there are more air currents to contend with. Use a fan that provides not less than 500 cubic feet of exchange per minute, and be sure there's an adequate air intake source.

You can also install a down-draft unit in an island. Check the manufacturer's specs and your local code for details about the proper size and installation method for the exhaust ducting.

Figure 1-13 C shows a different plan, but one that's equally functional. The corner sink offers the same advantages it did in Figure 1-12 C. The dead corners are both used, and the design follows all five of the basic rules for counters. (The island is opposite the hinges of the under-counter pantry.)

Bring Dead Corners to Life

The Full Lazy Susan

Make corner cabinet space useful with either half or full lazy Susan cabinets. Figure 1-14 shows a typical nuisance corner arrangement. To get at something at the back of an ordinary corner cabinet, you have to remove most of what's at the front of the cabinet. Then you have to replace everything you removed. And cleaning or lining that kind of cabinet shelf requires the agility of a contortionist.

The full lazy Susan requires 12 inches on each side of an internal corner. Manufactured units are made to those dimensions. You'll waste space if you allow any more. Figure 1-14 shows one type of full lazy Susan unit. The "doors" are attached to the shelves and aren't visible in the elevation drawing. You can't see the doors because they turn around a central shaft with the shelves.

Another type of lazy Susan has doors that aren't attached to the shelves. Instead, the two door sections

A Half lazy Susan concealed

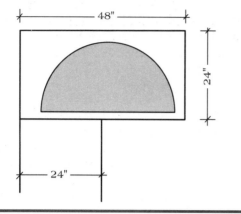

B Half lazy Susan rotated into the room

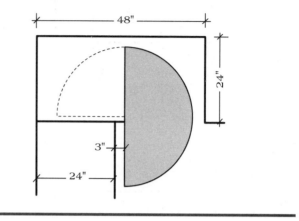

Figure 1-15
Half lazy Susan

are joined by hinges, and attached to one side of the opening with a piano hinge. Some lazy Susans rotate as a unit, while others allow you to rotate just one shelf at a time. Shelves are 8 to 10 inches apart, and in some cases, you can adjust the distance between them.

The Half Lazy Susan

The half lazy Susan provides about 2½ times more shelf space than the full lazy Susan, but it requires at least 24 inches of space from the internal corner on one side. Figure 1-15 A shows the unit when it's closed. Figure 1-15 B shows how the unit revolves into the room. These units are designed so they don't rotate past 90 degrees. So if you leave a 3-inch stile in the corner, the door handle won't strike the adjacent cabinet.

Figure 1-16 illustrates a half lazy Susan unit that pulls out of the cabinet so the entire half-round shelf extends into the room. The unit is supported by glides that let you pull it into the room once it's fully rotated to the open position.

Many cabinet manufacturers sell these units already installed in their base and wall cabinets. You can buy unassembled units through your builder's supply company and install them yourself. Feeny Manufacturing Company, P.O. Box 191, Muncie, IN 47308, is one manufacturer of cabinet accessories called "Cabineats" which include a variety of lazy Susans, bins, drawers, sliding shelves and space-saving storage units and hardware.

A Normal

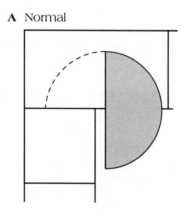

B Extended

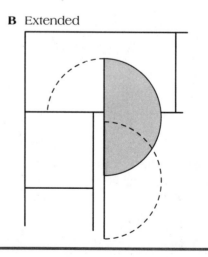

Figure 1-16
Half lazy Susan that extends fully into the room

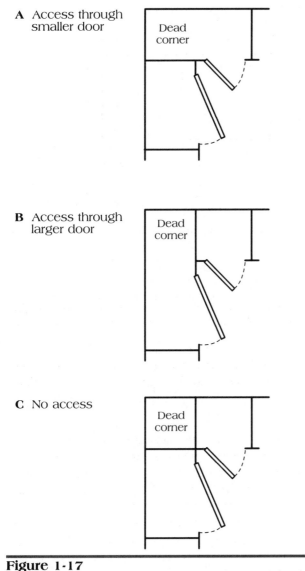

A Access through smaller door

Dead corner

B Access through larger door

Dead corner

C No access

Dead corner

Figure 1-17
Three ways to handle dead corner space in upper cabinets

If you don't have at least 24 inches on one leg of the corner for a half lazy Susan, you'll have to use the full lazy Susan instead. But remember, in this case, you'll need 12 inches of free space on both sides of the corner.

Dead Corners in Upper Cabinets

Corner wall cabinets have the same accessibility problem that corner base cabinets have. But the problem isn't quite as serious because wall cabinets aren't normally as deep as base cabinets. There are several ways to design around the access problem in wall cabinets.

But the plan in Figure 1-17 A isn't one of the ways. Here, access to the dead corner is through the smaller of the two cabinet doors. Figure 1-17 B would make the corner a little easier to reach. In Figure 1-17 C, neither of the wall cabinets extends into the corner, so the corner area is blanked out. You'd have to fill the space at the bottom of this void by extending the base of one of the cabinets, or by inserting a separate piece of shelving.

Figures 1-18 A, B, and C show three layouts for corner wall cabinets. The cabinet in Figure 1-18 A isn't very practical for storing things you have to reach often. It's hard to reach into the back of this cabinet, especially the upper shelves.

Figure 1-18 B shows a stand-alone carousel that allows access. True, you sacrifice a substantial part of the total shelf area, but the corner is good for tall, thin objects such as a jug or jar. With the layout in Figure 1-18 C you also lose some shelf space, but the space that remains is usable and easy to reach.

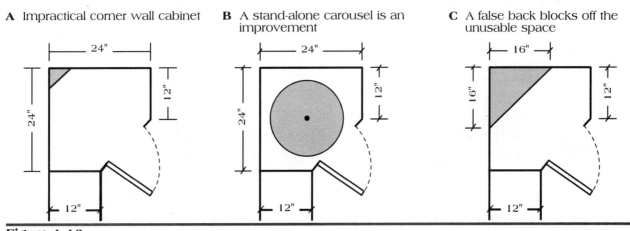

A Impractical corner wall cabinet

B A stand-alone carousel is an improvement

C A false back blocks off the unusable space

Figure 1-18
Three layouts for a corner wall cabinet

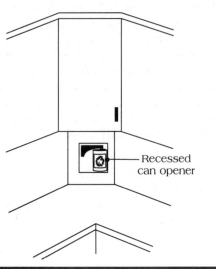

Figure 1-19
Use the dead space in a corner of the countertop

Extending the false back all the way down to the countertop provides room to recess a can opener, as shown in Figure 1-19. You could do the same thing under any of the cabinets in Figure 1-18.

Once I installed a wall safe in the space behind the cabinet in Figure 1-19 C. We put a touch-lock access door in the back of the cabinet to create an inconspicuous hiding place for small valuables.

Kitchens and Family Lifestyle

We've talked a lot about function so far, but when you design kitchens, you also have to consider the users' lifestyles. You'll have to be a guide, and sometimes the arbitrator as well. And where there are children involved, you'll have even more special needs and preferences to consider. Avoid designing the kitchen to meet your own requirements. Your job is to meet a clients' needs, not design around your own prejudices.

Learn as much as you can about your clients. How old are they? Do they have any physical limitations? Is there one major cook in the family, or do two or more family members use the kitchen at the same or different times? Do they want a seating-level counter or nook for quick meals?

Here are some more questions to ask:

◆ Which of the owner's present appliances will you reuse in the new kitchen design?

◆ What new appliances will you or the owners buy? Be sure you know the exact measurements of these appliances. Avoid surprises so the installer doesn't have to use fillers or alter any cabinets.

◆ Will the microwave oven be part of the wall oven or eye-level range, or a stand-alone?

◆ What kinds of small appliances do your clients use? Do they want them built into the wall or countertop? How much counter-level storage do they need for blenders, food processors, or mixers?

◆ Ask about special preferences for things like a spice drawer, wood or marble cutting board, wine rack, or display areas for fine china or stemware. Carefully consider the location of display cabinets and provide lighting if needed.

◆ Do your clients want a trash compactor, or would they prefer an inexpensive, energy-efficient, built-in trash bin finished to match the cabinets?

◆ Are there small children? Will the owners want a safe play area in or near the kitchen where they can keep a watchful eye on them while they cook? And do they need storage space for a high chair or other children's furniture?

◆ Should you arrange a place for a TV, radio, stereo or intercom? How about a desk with a shelf above for cookbooks? Where should the telephone go?

◆ Do your clients have a hobby they want to incorporate into their kitchen design? I once had a magazine gardening editor who wanted space in a small kitchen to show off and enjoy her plants and flowers. An inventive designer can find many suitable ways to meet that kind of challenge. One solution might be to install a garden window, a pop-out window containing shelves that extends beyond the wall of the building. Those are available in sizes to fit most window openings.

You can recess a planter box in the space behind a kitty-corner sink, or put one on top of a cabinet that doesn't reach all the way to the ceiling. If there's room, you might provide a floor-to-ceiling tension pole with brackets for potted plants, or hang them from hooks in the ceiling. You can also plan for display brackets, shelves, or niches to be built into masonry or conventional plaster walls. Your clients will appreciate any choices or alternatives you can suggest that will meet their special needs.

Client Preferences

I've noticed that my clients seem to have clear preferences about the location of their dishwashers that have nothing to do with whether they're right- or left-handed. If they've always had it on the right side of the sink, you'll probably have to arrange your design so it stays there. There's no use trying to convince them otherwise. It takes real diplomacy and persuasion to change a client's mind about something they feel very strongly about.

Some clients are partial to ideas that you might find unappealing. Once I had a client who insisted on having her dishes on open shelves so she could get at them without having to open doors, which of course made some sense. I tried to change her mind, explaining how dusty the dishes would get, but she was determined. So we built open shelves.

Occasionally, and I hope not often, you'll have a client who is picky about details to the point of being unreasonable. Learn to recognize that type at the beginning, or you'll have problems. I once placed a kitchen sink an inch off center of the window to make room for a lazy Susan in an otherwise useless corner. Most people wouldn't have even noticed. But this man did. He insisted that the sink be dead center before he'd make the next payment. There was nothing else to do but rework the waste line and make a new countertop to center the sink. That 1 inch cost me a bundle.

Be flexible enough to give your clients what they want, even if their wishes aren't entirely practical. For example, I've included island cabinets in kitchens that were too small simply because my clients demanded island cabinets. People who fancy themselves gourmet cooks seem to feel that work islands are essential, probably because gourmet cooks on TV always have work islands. And be sensitive to traditions. Some people's cooking habits are dictated by their religious or ethnic backgrounds – they may have special requirements for placement of the range top and oven, for example. In that case, be ready to bend the five Basic Rules a little.

When You Have to Move a Wall

If your kitchen redesign requires that you tear out a wall, you have to consider whether that wall supports the roof or upper floor. If there is an upstairs, and another wall is on top of the wall you want to move, it's almost certainly a loadbearing wall. In a single-story house, you have to go into the attic and examine the ceiling joists. If joists end at that wall, it's definitely a bearing wall. But often, the joists that span the wall in question extend on to rest on another wall. Is the wall in the middle helping support the joists? If you're not experienced in structural construction, you'd better consult with someone who is. One thing you don't want to do is mistake a loadbearing wall for a non-loadbearing one.

You can safely remove a non-loadbearing wall. But if you plan to remove a bearing wall, you have to provide support to take the place of the wall. Again, unless you're experienced in structural construction, you need the help of a professional.

Putting Your Ideas on Paper

Every kitchen design begins with a floor plan. Your plans have to be accurate scale drawings of what you propose. Otherwise you're likely to have some unpleasant surprises when work begins.

One way to make a scale drawing is to use graph paper, but that's not always the best way, especially if the room you're working with has angles that aren't square. Use an architect's scale rule instead. This isn't the same thing as an engineering scale rule. In an architect's rule, each major division (foot) is further divided into a multiple of 12 spaces to represent inches. An engineering scale, on the other hand, is divided decimally.

The Architect's Scale

The architect's rule has eleven scales. Two of the faces have two scales on each edge. The third face has two scales on one edge, and the #16 scale runs the full length of the other edge. The number at the end of each side of the rule shows the scale measurement. See the large number 1 at the left side of Figure 1-20. That indicates that the scale is 1 inch = 1 foot. The numbers 8, 7, and 6 refer to the number of ½ inch divisions, counting from the opposite end of the scale.

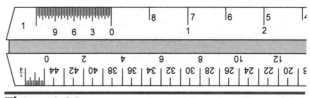

Figure 1-20

Architect's scale, with 1 inch = 1 foot scale at top left

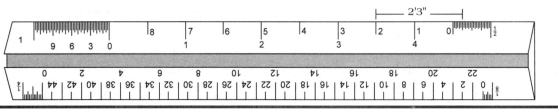

Figure 1-21
Transferring measurements using the 1/2 inch = 1 foot scale

If you want to transfer a measurement of 2 feet 3 inches to a sketch using the ½-inch scale, mark off the distance, as shown in Figure 1-21. Begin with the number 2 and measure back toward the 0, then beyond the 0 to the 3-inch mark. The resulting line is 2 feet 3 inches long, based on the ½ inch = 1 foot scale.

Taking Accurate Measurements

Here's how I measure a kitchen: Begin at the left end of the outside or window wall. Measure from left to right, from the corner to the first opening, whether that's a doorway or a window. Rule off a column along the right edge of a sheet of paper. At the top of the column, write "Wall A," and beneath that, write your first measurement. If the openings have trim around them, include the trim as part of the wall space, not part of the opening.

Now, measure the first opening, then the next wall space, and so on to the next corner. Draw a line, and then write the overall measurement for that wall, and label that measurement "O/A" so that later you won't think that's another wall or opening space.

When you change direction to a new wall, label that "Wall B." Continue around the room to your right, labeling each wall alphabetically, listing each wall space and opening as before. Later, when you transfer these measurements to your floor plan, you'll have all the information you need. Remember that mistakes can be very expensive.

When you lay out cabinets and counters on your plan, allow a clearance of ¼ inch to ½ inch from each wall. Walls are rarely perfectly square and plumb. It's easier to add a cover strip when you install cabinets than it is to cut them down to fit.

Figure 1-22 is a sketch and list of measurements from one of my kitchen jobs. Try to place your wall labels outside the plan area, and leave the inside for drawing your layout.

Use your sketch and list of measurements to draw the floor plan, or plan view, as shown in Figure 1-23. Section A shows both base and upper cabinets, while Section B shows base cabinets only.

Figure 1-24 contains elevation drawings of the same floor plan as Figure 1-23. The dotted lines on the floor plan labeled "Elev. (A)" and "Elev. (B)" match the same labels on the elevation drawings.

On the elevation drawings, the spaces marked with a large X are cross sections of the cabinets which appear on the elevations for the walls that join these. The horizontal lines across the cabinet sections indicate the number and location of the shelves inside.

When you prepare your drawings, leave space on the page for general notes. Number those notes, and then put the same number in a circle on the sketch itself, to show where each item goes. That's where you'd describe special items like a bread keeper, silverware or cutlery drawer, lazy Susan, or sliding shelves, if there isn't room for those labels on the sketch itself.

Symbols for Plan Drawings

Use common construction drawing symbols to give your plans a more professional appearance. People who work from your plans will appreciate anything you do to clarify what's expected of them. Figure 1-25 shows the following drawing symbols:

◆ Indicate windows with two horizontal lines, not one. Use the same symbol for all kinds of windows, and describe them with detail notes.

◆ Don't draw wall lines through doorways. Leave the space between the jambs clear.

◆ Show sliding patio (Arcadia) doors with two bypassing lines. When you show sliding doors this way, you must draw by-passing windows with two lines so they won't be mistaken for patio doors.

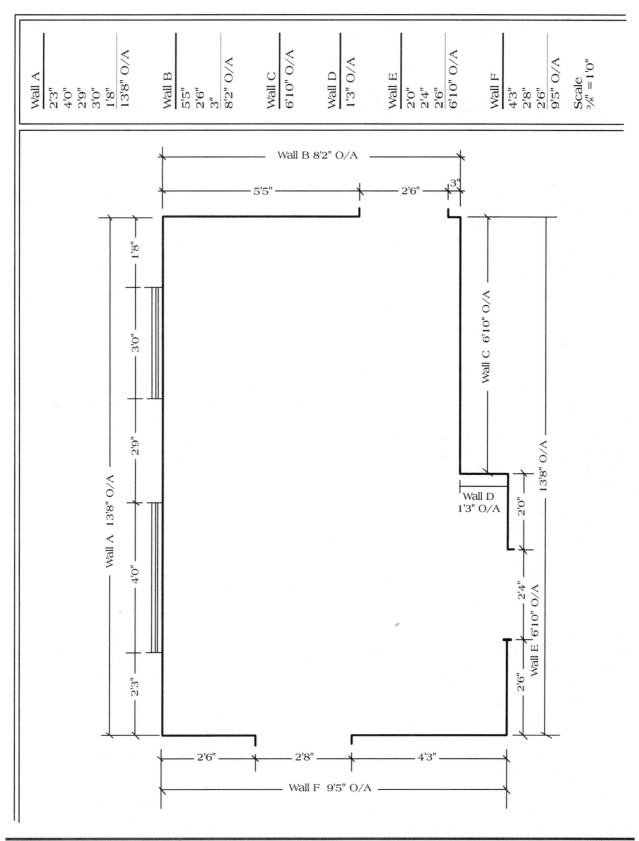

Figure 1-22
Room measurements and floor plan layout

A Plan view showing wall and base cabinets

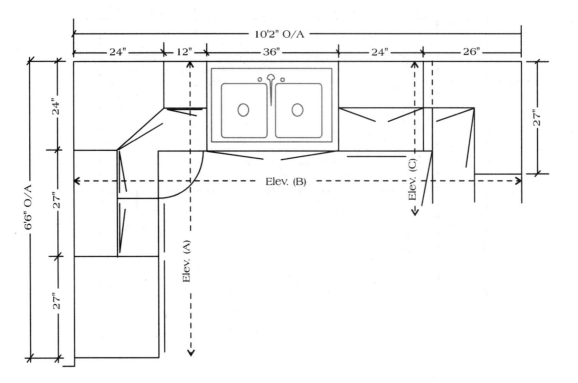

B Plan view showing only base cabinets

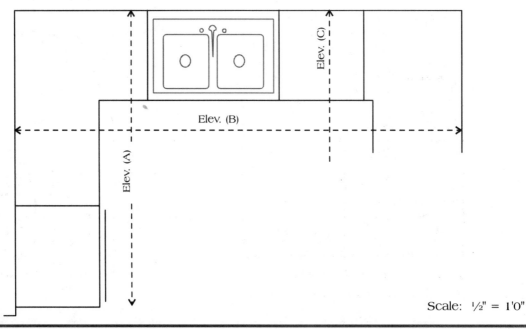

Scale: ½" = 1'0"

Figure 1-23
Typical plan views

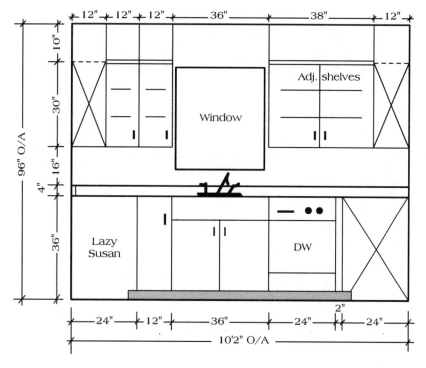

Elev. (B)

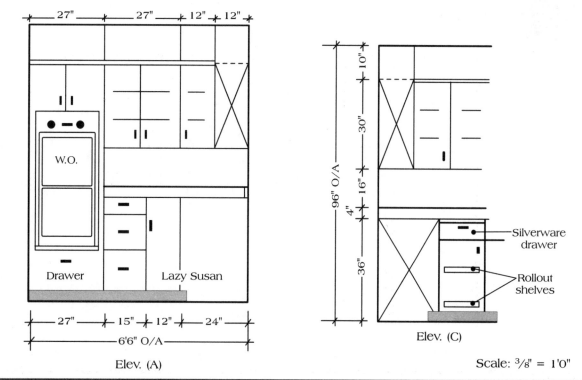

Elev. (A)

Elev. (C)

Scale: ³⁄₈" = 1'0"

Figure 1-24
Elevation views

◆ Show pocket doors as a double dashed line, and be sure the wall that will contain the open door is long enough to conceal it. Also, be certain that there aren't any electrical or plumbing runs inside the wall where you plan to install the door. Pipe and conduit can be moved, but only at extra expense.

◆ Dotted wall lines indicate wall area to be removed. Show walls to be added with a series of lines parallel to the wall face.

It's not my purpose to give you a basic course in drafting here. But if you're a designer working with a contractor, you must make sure the contractor knows exactly what you want done. Make plenty of notes on your drawings, and describe everything in complete detail.

In the chapters that follow, we'll discuss several different kitchen floor plans. I'll show you how to arrange the work triangle for each of them, and warn of the pitfalls common to each arrangement.

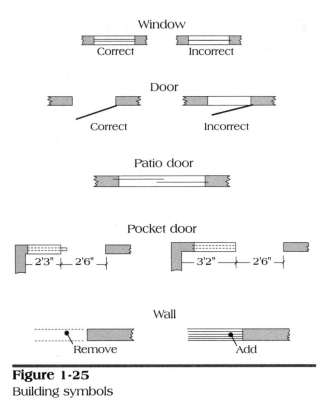

Figure 1-25
Building symbols

Test Questions for Chapter 1

1. When designing a kitchen, what should be your prime objective?

2. What are the five Basic Rules for counter placement?

3. What's the minimum counter space you should allow between the sink and a major cooking appliance?

4. Why should you never place the cooktop at the end of a counter?

5. Why is it important to have a pantry cabinet in the kitchen?

6. What can you do to make better use of hard-to-reach or dead corners so often found in kitchens?

7. Why is it important to know the lifestyle of your client before you begin planning the kitchen?

8. Why is it best to use an architect's scale, rather than an engineer's scale, when you're preparing scale drawings of your kitchen design?

9. Why is it helpful to have a correctly-measured room layout prepared before beginning to plan the kitchen?

10. Why should you know and use the standard construction symbols in any plans you draw?

CHAPTER 2
The Compact Kitchen

All compact kitchens are small, but not all small kitchens are compact. At least, not if you agree that compact implies an efficient use of space. In this chapter, we'll look at design features that allow you to make an efficient and attractive kitchen when you only have a small space to work with. We'll start with the most difficult design – the one-wall kitchen.

The One-Wall Kitchen

In a one-wall kitchen, the designer has to use every inch effectively, and yet stick to all the Basic Rules. You'll usually find these kitchens at the end of a multi-purpose room, or on the wall opposite a serving or eating counter. They must contain all the elements of their larger counterparts – work space, cooking appliances, refrigeration, storage, and ventilation – but in a very limited area. You can put a fully functional one-wall kitchen into a space just 15 feet long, and you can do it with standard, full-sized appliances.

The best one-wall kitchen design has the sink in the center, and the range and refrigerator at opposite ends. Placement of the refrigerator depends upon which way it opens. Remember, you need counter space on the side opposite the hinges.

You need to pay particular attention to storage and convenience in a small kitchen. Provide adjustable shelves in the upper cabinets, and roll-out shelves in the lower ones. In a kitchen like this, you can't afford any wasted space.

Lighting can be a problem is this kitchen design. Of course, the range hood should contain an exhaust fan and a light. But someone working at the counter may be standing in their own shadow if the ceiling light is any distance behind them. Install small fluorescent fixtures beneath the upper cabinets where necessary to brighten the countertop. Choose lights designed especially for mounting under cabinets, only about an inch high.

Figure 2-1 shows a single-wall kitchen like you would find in many smaller homes and efficiency apartments. "W" indicates wall cabinets and "B" shows base cabinets. Figure 2-2 is the elevation view of Figure 2-1. The horizontal lines in the cabinets indicate placement of the shelves.

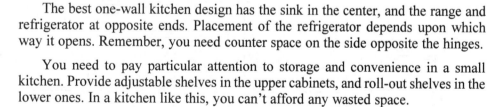

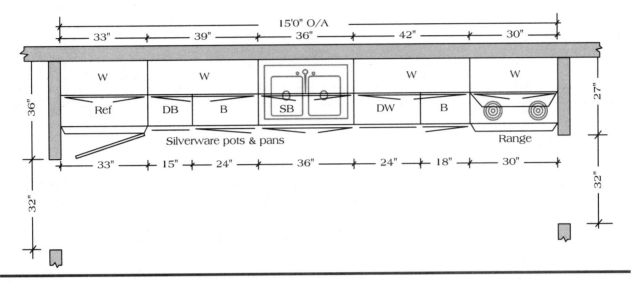

Figure 2-1
This one-wall kitchen is backwards

At first glance, this kitchen seems to have enough cabinet space and countertops. But study it for a minute and I think you'll agree that it's very poorly planned.

Of the three Basic Rules that apply to this arrangement, only Rule 1, counter space on both sides of the sink, has been followed. The refrigerator opens on the wrong side, and there's a wall immediately beside the range top. There's adequate space between

the sink and the range, but part of that space will often be cluttered with dirty dishes, or the dish drainer.

In Figure 2-3, the size of the kitchen is exactly the same, with the same full-size appliances. We switched the refrigerator to the other end of the room to allow for counter space next to the door opening.

There are base cabinets on both sides of the range to hold pots, pans, measuring and stirring utensils. The cabinets have roll-out shelves to make it easy to

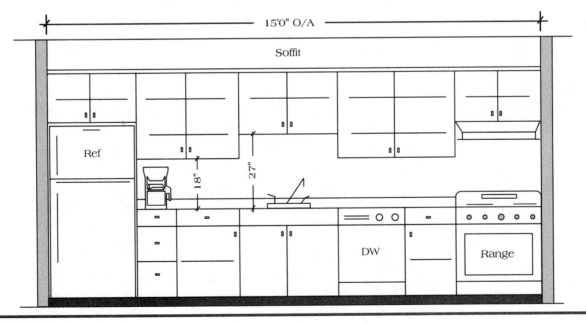

Figure 2-2
Elevation view of Figure 2-1

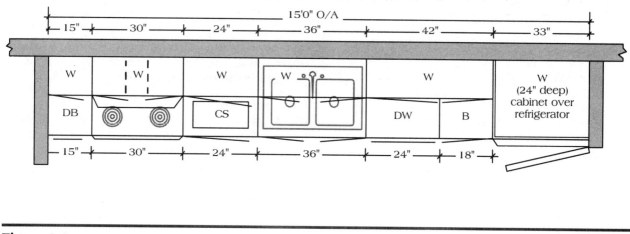

Figure 2-3
Same appliances, better arrangement

get at bulky or heavy pans. There's also a roll-out shelf in the bottom of the sink cabinet. The roll-out shelves are indicated with a shallow rectangle in the elevation view in Figure 2-4.

There's a built-in, eye-level microwave oven beside the range, and a counter saver (indicated with a CS) built into the countertop where one can set hot pans from either cooking appliance. Be sure to include that if the counter surface is plastic laminate, or other material which won't withstand heat. It can be made of ceramic tile, granite, or Corian. There's a pull-out cutting board in the cabinet next to the refrigerator.

Notice the short cabinet over the sink in Figure 2-2. In Figure 2-4 you can see we've made that cabinet full length to regain that most important lower shelf. Where space is limited, you can install a narrow shelf

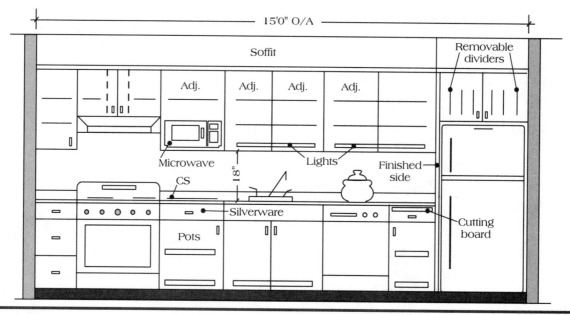

Figure 2-4
Elevation view of 2-3

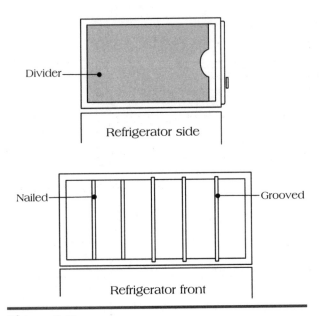

Divider

Refrigerator side

Nailed —●— Grooved

Refrigerator front

Figure 2-5
Tray storage above refrigerator

a few inches below a wall cabinet to hold spice containers or other small items.

It's customary to make the cabinet over the refrigerator the same depth as the other wall cabinets, as you see it in Figure 2-1. In Figure 2-4 we've enlarged the cabinet over the refrigerator so it's 24 inches deep instead of 18 inches. Now you can install a series of adjustable vertical dividers where the homeowner can store trays, cookie sheets and other flat objects.

Figure 2-5 illustrates how to outfit that cabinet. Use thin sheets of plywood, Masonite, plastic, or pressed board for the dividers. Shape the front end of the dividers to make it easy to grasp the items stored between them. You can use a router to make grooves in the top and bottom of the cabinet for the dividers to ride in. Or you can fasten strips of quarter-round molding to the cabinet top and bottom to hold the dividers in place.

Unless the refrigerator is the exact width of the space allowed for it, there's a narrow opening on one or both sides of it. That space is a nuisance to clean, and seems to attract little things like pens, pencils, silverware and small toys. All of those things are hard to remove without a lot of effort and a pointed stick.

You can solve this problem by enclosing the refrigerator in a cabinet. Use ¾-inch material to match the rest of the cabinets and extend it to the ceiling. In Figure 2-4, this cabinet wall also encloses the deep cabinet above the refrigerator. This treatment

gives a free-standing refrigerator the appearance of a much more expensive built-in unit.

Leave at least ¾-inch clearance on each side of the box so it can be pulled out when necessary for repair or cleaning. If the refrigerator you're installing doesn't have casters, place it on a dolly that's made for that purpose.

You may also need to allow for ventilation above the refrigerator. Many refrigerators with exposed coils on the back require ventilation at the top so heat can escape. Otherwise the compressor motor may run continually and even burn out. Some models are vented at the front through a grille at the base and can be fully enclosed in a cabinet or alcove. Check the specifications of the refrigerator you're installing to determine how much ventilation it requires and how much space you must allow at the sides and top.

If space is extremely limited, you can buy appliances in narrow widths. Dishwashers come 18 inches wide, and refrigerators as small as 24 inches. You can also find counter-high refrigerators which would be adequate for a single person, and would leave space for a pantry cabinet above it.

The Two-Wall Kitchen

The two-wall kitchen is designed around a corridor that's open at both ends. It's very compact, and can be functional or not, depending on the arrangement of the appliances on the two walls.

The passage space in a corridor kitchen can be as narrow as 36 inches between base cabinet faces, but provide at least 48 inches if possible.

Because the space in these kitchens is generally so limited, they provide a special challenge to the designer. You need to pay special attention to the Basic Rules for counter space. You also have to avoid hazardous traffic patterns.

Figure 2-6 shows a kitchen that follows the Basic Rules, but it's still is a poorly-planned kitchen. There are two problems with placement of the dishwasher and wall oven. First, you can't open both of them at the same time, or stand in front of one while the other is open. And their doors are dangerously close to the entry.

Note Figure 2-7. We moved the appliances to allow use of each of them without interference from the other. The appliances with doors hinged on the bottom are no longer opposite one another. Nor does either of them open into a doorway.

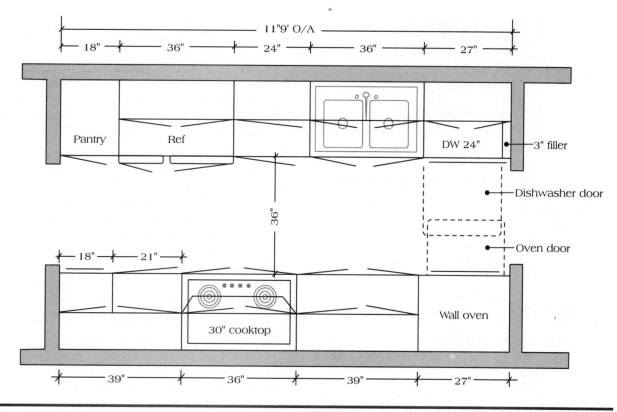

Figure 2-6
This corridor kitchen needs help

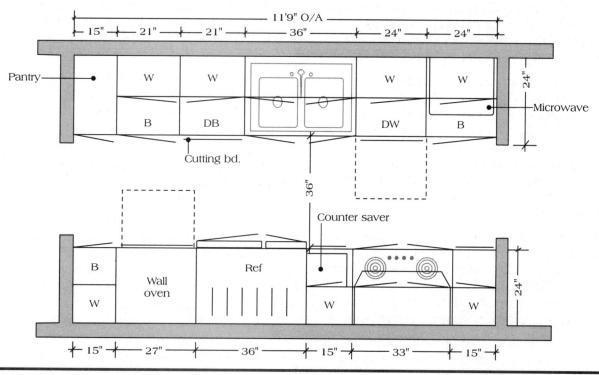

Figure 2-7
Here's a better corridor arrangement

Unfortunately, there's another potentially danger-ous problem lurking here. Carrying a hot pan from the range top or wall oven to the sink requires crossing the passageway. The solution: Put the cooktop on the same side of the kitchen as the sink.

Where there's enough room between two walls of a corridor kitchen, Figure 2-8 shows an ideal arrange-ment. Here, we've used a free-standing range instead of the cooktop and wall oven. The oven door is far enough into the room so that someone entering the kitchen will see it in time to avoid running into it, and it's also protected by the extended wall. The range is now on the same side as the sink so there's no danger of the cook colliding with someone passing through. The dishwasher door doesn't extend into the door-way.

Figures 2-9 and 2-10 are elevation views of Figure 2-8. You can see that this kitchen, despite being very compact, is still both attractive and func-tional. Even without a window, there's plenty of light due to ceiling and under-cabinet lighting. There's room for a counter saver next to the range and beneath the microwave oven. On the opposite wall, both the refrigerator and the pantry have counter space in the proper location.

As in the one-wall kitchen, we've put roll-out shelves in the base cabinets, and the lower part of the pantry. Avoid installing roll-out shelves above eye level. You still won't be able to see what's on them when they're pulled out. There's tray storage over the refrigerator, and adjustable shelves in the upper cabi-nets.

An alternative arrangement would be to separate the refrigerator from the pantry, putting them at oppo-site ends of the wall. Use a refrigerator with the freez-er on the top or bottom, and locate it at the end of the kitchen nearest the sink. Be sure the door opens so there's counter space at the open side. This offers an

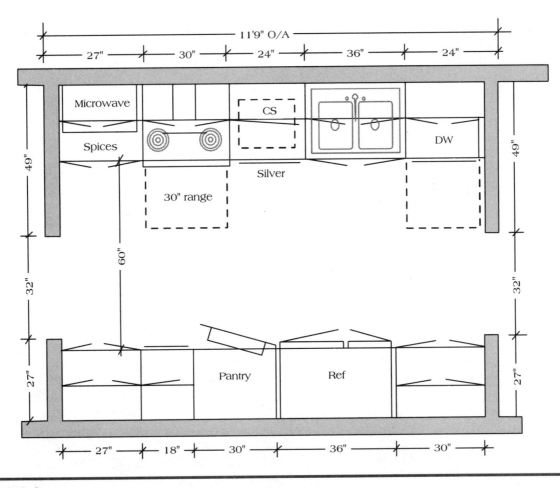

Figure 2-8
A larger corridor kitchen allows for an ideal layout

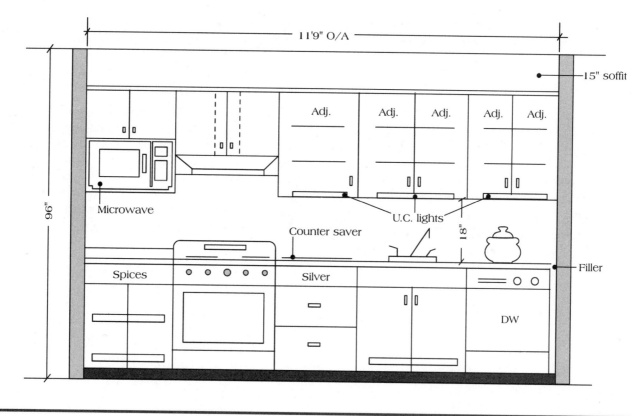

Figure 2-9

Elevation view, sink side of Figure 2-8

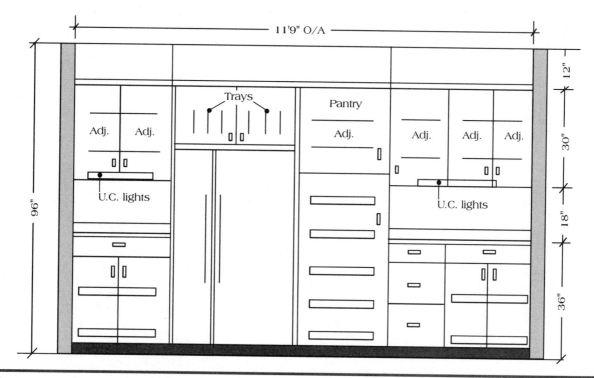

Figure 2-10

Elevation view, refrigerator side of Figure 2-8

added advantage of providing an unbroken expanse of counter space between the pantry and refrigerator.

A Word About Dishwashers

In a small kitchen, you may need to place the dishwasher between the sink cabinet and a wall as we did here. Remember to support the countertop at the wall end. Place the dishwasher at least 2 inches from the wall, and use a filler strip to conceal the support. I once had a job where this wasn't done. When a worker tried to stand on the counter before the dishwasher was installed, the countertop collapsed. That was an expensive mistake. Fortunately, the worker wasn't hurt, or it would have been even more expensive.

. . . And Bread Boxes

If you install a bread keeper in a base cabinet, don't put it next to the dishwasher unless you provide adequate insulation in the cabinet. Dishwashers aren't insulated for either heat or steam, and either one reaching the bread box would probably cause the bread to become moldy. You can put a bread box next to an oven, however, because ranges and ovens have enough insulation to prevent the problem.

Test Questions for Chapter 2

1. Why is it difficult to design a functional one-wall kitchen?

2. What is the best arrangement for the refrigerator and the range in a one-wall kitchen?

3. Although ceiling lights provide good general lighting, they cause a person at the counter to be working in his or her own shadow. What can you do to eliminate this problem?

4. How can you maximize the storage space in a very small kitchen?

5. How can you add more storage space without extending the length of the present walls or changing the present layout?

6. How can you make the space under the sink more useful?

7. In a corridor kitchen, what's the minimum passage space you should allow between base cabinet faces?

8. What two major appliances should not be placed opposite each other in a narrow kitchen?

9. In a corridor kitchen, as long as there's ample space, as shown in Figure 2-8, why is it better to place the range on the same side as the sink?

10. When a dishwasher is to be installed at the end of a counter, and will support it, why is it advisable to provide some independent end support?

CHAPTER 3
The L-Shaped Kitchen

It's harder to create a functional design in an L-shaped kitchen than in a single-wall or a corridor (two-wall) kitchen. The walls meet at a right angle, creating a potentially useless corner. But even with an L-shaped kitchen, keeping the five Basic Rules and the work triangle in mind can produce excellent results.

All the examples in this book come from my own experience, from the kitchens and homes I've worked in during my professional career. After working with hundreds of homes and hundreds of owners, I've learned that no two homes, no two kitchens, can or should be alike. That's because people are different. What's a sensible solution for the Jones family won't work for the Smith family next door. Everyone has unique needs and desires. It's your job to design a kitchen to serve those needs and desires. Maybe that's what makes this business so interesting. What works today may not work tomorrow. A kitchen designer should approach every job as an opportunity to find creative answers to meet special needs.

But even though every kitchen can be unique, many share the same design flaws. Figure 3-1 shows a kitchen with far more than its share of problems. Before reading any further, spend a few minutes to pick out the problems in Figure 3-1. List at least six flaws on a piece of paper. Then read on and compare your list with mine.

◆ First, the range is adjacent to the pantry, where it presents a fire hazard, or at least the danger of scorching the wood cabinet. Also, the heat may affect some of the groceries stored in the pantry, and there's no place for the pot handles on the left side of the range top. This design violates both Rules 2 and 5: Counters are necessary on both sides of the range, and on at least one side of the pantry.

◆ The sink cabinet next to the angle of the L produces a dead corner. The position of the sink prevents placement of a full lazy Susan. But there is room for a half lazy Susan instead of the conventional base cabinet.

◆ There's no cabinet or drawer space near the dishwasher. And remember, there must be a filler or end wall next to the refrigerator to support the countertop.

◆ The refrigerator opens the wrong way. The cabinet above it is of little use because it's so small and hard to reach.

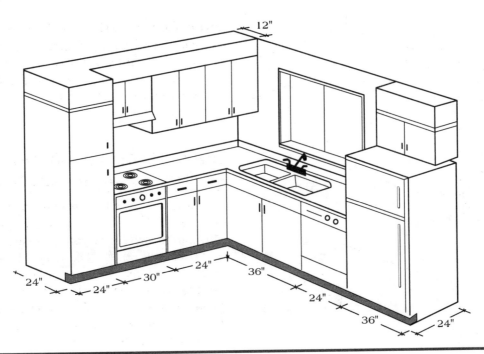

Figure 3-1
Inefficient design for an L-shaped kitchen

◆ There's wasted space where additional cabinets could be installed on both sides of the window.

◆ The kitchen looks chopped up without a valance to connect the two soffit sections.

The overall dimensions of this kitchen are only 8½ by 10 feet. It's amazing that such a small kitchen could have so many things wrong with it. But the designer could have avoided all those errors by sticking to the Basic Rules.

Add a Valance

Let's start by tying the kitchen together. Installing a valance over the window creates continuity. A kitchen shouldn't be a random collection of shapes, lines, textures and colors. It should reflect harmony and unity. Adding a valance connects the two sides of the window. And the valance will conceal a light fixture that's needed in this kitchen.

The height of the valance is critical. It can't extend below the soffit, or you won't be able to open the cabinet door at the left of the window. And, if you make it too short, it looks skimpy and doesn't hide the light fixture. To look best, the valance should be the same depth as the soffits on each side of it, and extend to the ceiling. See Figure 3-2.

On the Subject of Soffits

Soffits make a high-ceiling room seem cozier. They also make a room seem wider. Modern kitchens often feature dropped ceilings or soffits, either to bring the upper cabinets within reach, or to conceal lighting fixtures, air conditioning, plumbing, or electrical installations. When the soffit is confined to the

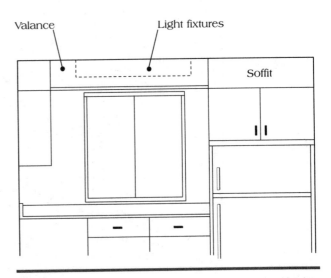

Figure 3-2
Use a valance to unify a poor design

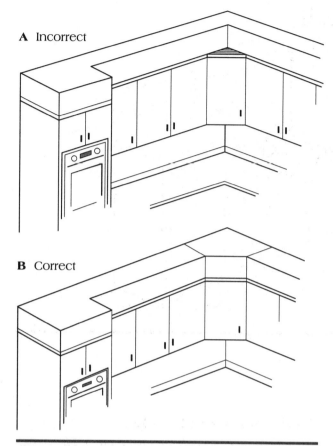

A Incorrect

B Correct

Figure 3-3
Soffit must follow shape of cabinet beneath it

edge of the room, design it so that it follows the shape of the cabinets it covers. Figure 3-3 shows why this is necessary. When the soffit doesn't fill up the space above the cabinet, the exposed section over the kitty-corner cabinet is a dust collector.

Solving the Problems of Our Example Kitchen

There are a couple of ways to improve the kitchen in Figure 3-1. One way is shown in Figure 3-4. Moving the sink to the corner creates enough space on the outside wall for the range. That shortens the range exhaust vent to the exterior. For convenience, we put a counter to the right of the left-opening refrigerator. And we put a cabinet above the dishwasher. There's also a bank of drawers next to the sink to hold silverware, utensils, and towels.

The Indented Sink Cabinet

The sink was indented to make more room for the person using the dishwasher. That also makes it easier to reach the corner behind the sink. Notice the 5-inch filler between the dishwasher and the sink cabinet. That provides even more room in front of the sink when the dishwasher door is open.

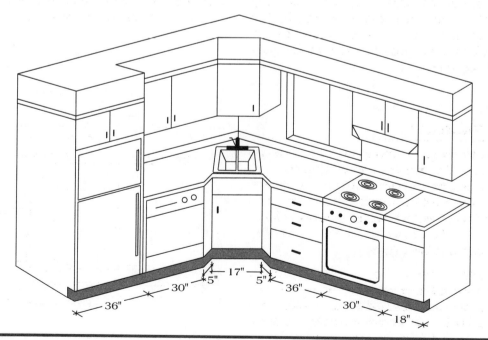

Figure 3-4
An efficient solution to the poor design

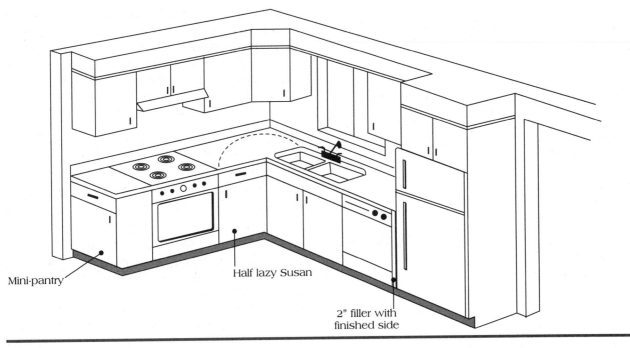

Mini-pantry

Half lazy Susan

2" filler with
finished side

Figure 3-5
Another solution to the poor design

If You Can Change
the Refrigerator Door

If the refrigerator in Figure 3-1 had opened to the right, I would have made the changes shown in Figure 3-5. Figure 3-6 is a plan view of part of Figure 3-5.

The sink stays in front of the window. The half lazy Susan solves the dead corner problem. The mini-pantry provides a countertop next to the range. There's a 2-inch filler between the dishwasher and the refrigerator to provide end support for the countertop. And the cabinet over the refrigerator is as deep as the refrigerator to make use of wasted space. There's also a wall cabinet over the dishwasher, and the upper corner cabinet provides additional storage for dishes and glassware. There are drawers over the lazy Susan and in the pantry cabinet.

Avoid Moving Windows
If You Can

What if you don't have enough space for the half lazy Susan? The sink doesn't have to go directly in front of the window. Remember, a half lazy Susan requires 24 inches of exposed cabinet on only one side of the corner, while a full lazy Susan requires 12

inches on *both* sides. The only way to recover this wasted corner is to move the sink, as in Figure 3-7. Now there's room for the full lazy Susan. Notice that you can do this easily as long as the waste stub remains within the sink cabinet.

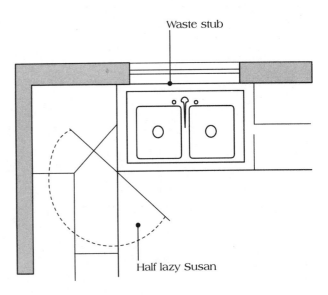

Waste stub

Half lazy Susan

Figure 3-6
Plan view of sink and half lazy Susan

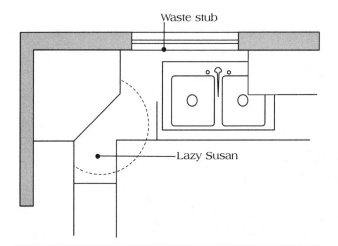

Figure 3-7
Upper cabinet hangs over offset sink . . .

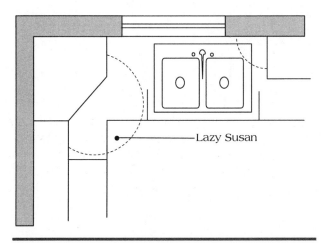

Figure 3-8
. . . But cabinet can be cut down

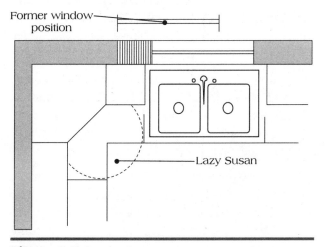

Figure 3-9
You could move the sink *and* window

But now there's another problem, as you can see in Figure 3-7. Assuming there's enough counter space to move the sink (and still leave room for the dishwasher), the upper cabinet would extend over the sink. You could cut the cabinet down, filling the open wall space with a small rectangular or quarter-round shelf or decorative sconces. See Figure 3-8.

If you decide to move the window, your finished wall will look like Figure 3-9. The shading shows where you'd fill in the wall section beside the window. Now there's space for another upper cabinet on the left side of the window.

The Odd-Shaped L Kitchen

Figure 3-10 is an L-shaped kitchen with some of the major appliances on a separate wall opposite the L. You can see from the elevation drawings in Figure 3-11 that this kitchen has many of the design problems we've been discussing. Let's check off a few of those problems:

◆ Dead corner created by the range top location

◆ Dead corner in upper cabinets as well

◆ Break in the soffit over the window

◆ Counter on wrong side of refrigerator

◆ Refrigerator butts to a projecting wall

◆ Shallow cabinet over refrigerator wastes space

And there's one more design flaw we haven't seen before. Notice the cabinet doors under the wall oven. That space would be useless to anyone but an acrobat. That cabinet should be a drawer.

One small structural change will allow us to greatly improve this kitchen.

When Structural Changes Are Required

In this case, a small change in wall layout let us make this kitchen work much better. We simply moved the doorway beside the range top 15 inches to the left.

That makes room for a lazy Susan in the base cabinet and a turntable in the corner cabinet above. We also used a 30-inch range hood, even though the range

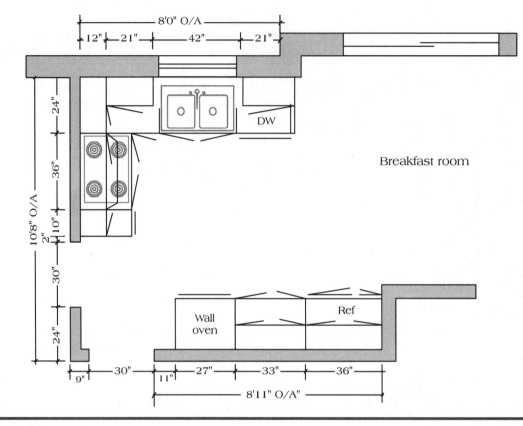

Figure 3-10
An L kitchen with an extra wall

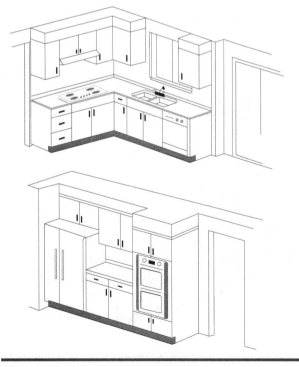

Figure 3-11
Elevations of Figure 3-10

is 36 inches wide. That lets us use larger wall cabinets on each side of the range.

On the wall opposite the L, we switched the positions of the wall oven and the refrigerator, making the countertop more usable. You can see from the plan view (Figure 3-12) that there's plenty of clearance at each of the doorways. We did that by putting a shallow canned goods cabinet next to the refrigerator, and by cutting down the cabinet between the wall oven and the refrigerator from 33 to 24 inches.

Figure 3-13 shows elevation views of both parts of this much-improved kitchen. Notice the decorative valance over the sink and the soffit that extends between the wall oven and the refrigerator. Both of those provide a place for concealed lighting.

It's usually not difficult or expensive to move a door opening in a non-structural wall. It's harder to make changes in loadbearing or masonry walls. If you're not an expert at framing, get advice from someone who is before you promise to make changes in structural walls.

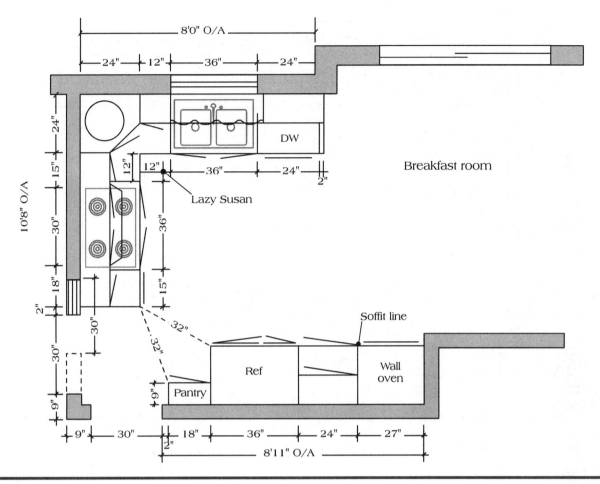

Figure 3-12
New arrangements for Figure 3-10

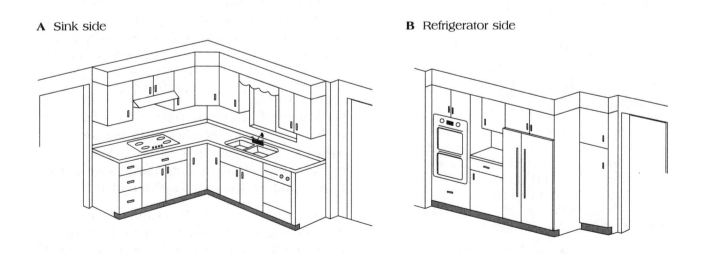

A Sink side

B Refrigerator side

Figure 3-13
Elevations of Figure 3-12

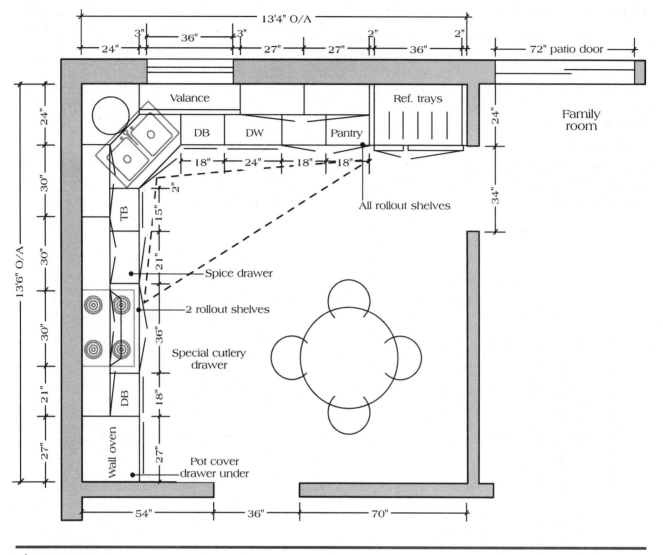

Figure 3-14
A spacious L kitchen

The Practically Perfect L-Shaped Kitchen...

When you have the luxury of designing a kitchen from scratch, you have flexibility that's often lacking in remodeling jobs. In Figure 3-14, there's plenty of space on both legs of the L – about 13½ feet – to provide a spacious, functional design. This kitchen is located conveniently for both the dining room and family room, and still has room for an eating area.

The kitty-corner sink is at the top of the work triangle with the refrigerator and cooktop at the other two points. There's over 36 inches of countertop between the sink and the range, and 6½ feet on the refrigerator side. The two 27-inch cabinets have plenty of storage space for dishes near the dishwasher, and the divided cabinet above the refrigerator holds trays, platters and cookie sheets. For an even nicer touch, make the dividers removable. Then if there's a tray too long to fit, the homeowner can remove one or two dividers and put it in on a slant. There's more space for utensils above the wall oven, and a drawer for pot covers below.

Under the sink, there's a large slide-out shelf for detergents and a slide-out towel rack. Next to the sink there's space for a trash bin or trash compactor. Base cabinets have roll-out shelves, there are special drawers to organize utensils, and the corner design makes efficient, accessible use of the space.

Even a tiny kitchen can be fully functional. In Figure 3-15, we put an L-shaped kitchen into a space that's only 6'7" by 9'3". We had to use compact fixtures and fudge a little on the Basic Rules to make everything fit. But this kitchen has all the necessary elements, and some innovations, too.

There's a microwave which incorporates a vent beneath the cabinet over the range. These are 30 inches wide, so you'd use 15-inch-wide upper cabinets to flank the microwave.

The primary disadvantage of a kitchen this size, as you might expect, is limited counter space. We had to settle for only 18 inches between the sink and the cooktop, but even that space is enough for a small dish drainer. (Several companies manufacture dishwashers that are only 18 inches wide.) Notice that the sink is a compact 24 inches, installed into a 27-inch base.

You could even have a window over the sink in a kitchen this small. If you restrict the window to 24 inches square there's still room for a 16-inch-high cabinet above the window.

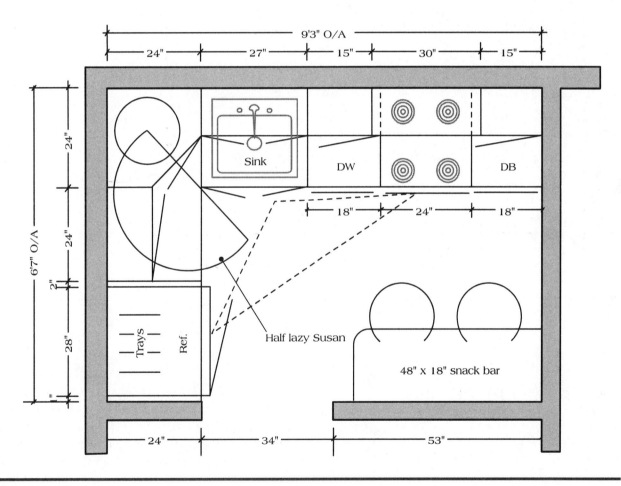

Figure 3-15
A very compact L kitchen

Test Questions for Chapter 3

1. How would you visually unify the kitchen shown in Figure 3-1? What other benefit does this change provide?

2. Why is it important that the soffits conform to the shapes of all the upper cabinets?

3. In the kitchen shown in Figure 3-4, what is the benefit of indenting the sink cabinet?

4. The space under a wall oven is, in most kitchens, accessible only if you're an acrobat. How can you make it more usable?

5. In Figure 3-10, the wall oven is 11 inches away from the doorway. Why is that?

6. How did moving the refrigerator from its position in Figure 3-10 to the position in Figure 3-11 improve its usefulness?

7. Why was it necessary to move the refrigerator at least 20 inches from the doorway?

8. Point out two good design features in the kitchen in Figure 3-14.

9. Is it possible to install a small pantry in a kitchen this size without losing any counter space?

10. What's the advantage of using a 24-inch-square window over the sink in the compact kitchen in Figure 3-15?

CHAPTER 4
The U-Shaped Kitchen

The U-shaped kitchen is probably the most popular. It's the one you usually see in the "Beautiful Kitchen" magazines. But it needs a good-sized room. Don't consider putting one in an area that's less than 8 feet wide.

Because the U-shaped kitchen has three walls to work with, it's the easiest to design as far as following the Basic Rules is concerned. With the opportunity to have the refrigerator on one wall, the range on another, and the sink on the third, it's easy to design a practical work triangle. As long as you keep the total distance around the triangle to 21 feet or less, you can't go wrong. Of course, when you're working with a remodel, which will be most of the time, you've got to adapt what's already there.

If you get to design a U-shaped kitchen from scratch, the first decision is deciding where to put the main components – the sink, the stove, the dishwasher and the refrigerator. If there's a picture window, that's the best place for the sink. Now you have a base point from which to figure the placement of the other parts of your ideal kitchen. Of course the dishwasher needs to be by the sink.

Then you have to place the refrigerator. For this, consider where the customer will be entering the kitchen with armloads of groceries to put away. They won't want to circle the whole kitchen, trip over the dishwasher door, then balance the groceries on their knee with one hand while they try to put a 20-pound turkey in the freezer compartment with the other. The best place for the refrigerator is near the sink, with its door hinged on the side opposite its adjacent countertop.

Next is the range. Put the range on the wall opposite the refrigerator, again making sure there's plenty of counter space on both sides of it.

My favorite U-shaped kitchen began as an L-shaped kitchen. Note Figure 4-1. It was cramped, and counter space was nearly nonexistent. We made this inconvenient kitchen much more functional by moving the patio door to the corner of the room and using the third wall.

Figure 4-2 shows the new design. Both corners now have easy-to-reach storage space, thanks to the lazy Susans and carousels.

We extended the upper cabinet to full depth over the refrigerator and built a pantry cabinet next to it. Once the patio door was moved, we had room for larger base and wall cabinets on both sides of the range and more counter space between the range and the sink.

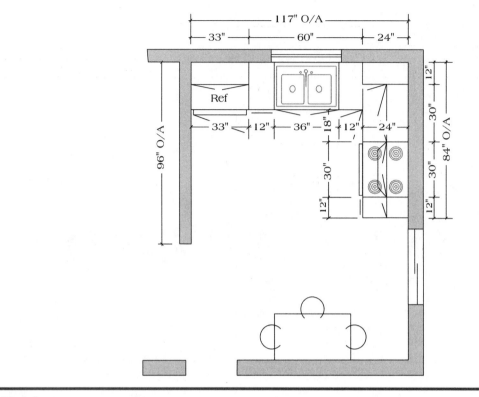

Figure 4-1
The L kitchen that shouldn't be

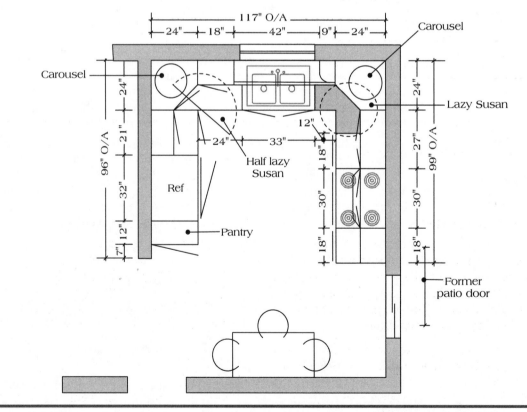

Figure 4-2
The L turned into a U

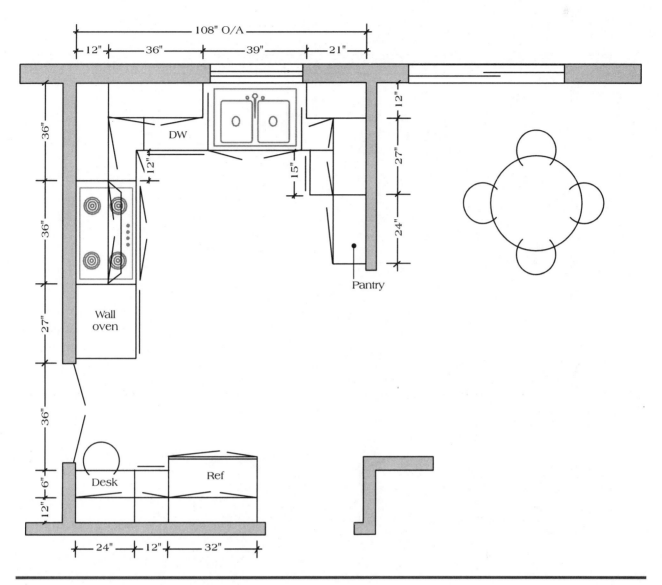

Figure 4-3
A U with an end wall, before remodel

Lighting Is Important

This kitchen has a light panel installed in a dropped ceiling, but it's still a good idea to provide a light over the sink. If there's a window over the sink, as shown in Figure 4-2, install a light fixture under the soffit, behind a valance. This brings the light source as close as possible to the countertop.

When there's no window, use an under-cabinet fixture above the sink. They're specially made for this purpose, and are only about an inch high. Conceal the fixture behind a lip on the cabinet face. The lip should extend at least an inch below the cabinet's lower shelf.

The U Kitchen with an End Wall

It's not unusual to find a U-shaped kitchen with another wall near the open end of the U. Figure 4-3 shows a kitchen before we redesigned it. The most obvious flaw was the location of the refrigerator so far from the sink. You'll spot several other errors we've already discussed. Nearly all are violations of the Basic Rules.

Notice one major inconvenience. The family had to walk around the pantry wall to get to the eating area. That's where we made the major changes.

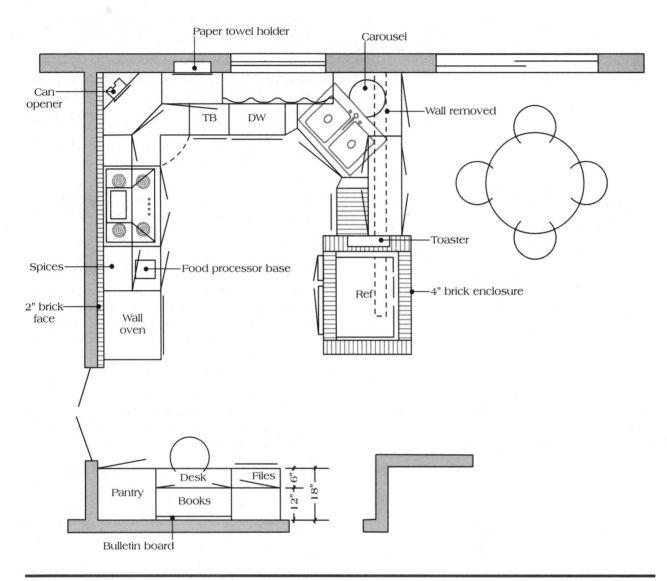

Figure 4-4
Moving the refrigerator improved this design

The Improved Kitchen Works

The wall between the kitchen and the breakfast room wasn't a loadbearing wall. We removed it and replaced it with cabinets and an enclosure for the refrigerator.

This refrigerator has an icemaker, so we ran the ¼-inch copper water line from the sink's water supply, beneath the cabinets to the refrigerator enclosure. You can also run the line under the base cabinet toe space. Of course, you install a shutoff valve under the sink to allow for repairing or moving the refrigerator.

Figure 4-4 is the floor plan of the revised kitchen. Most of the changes are obvious, but we'll discuss some of them in detail.

We'll begin with the wall oven and work clockwise around the room. We didn't move the wall oven – it was OK where it was. But it didn't have a counter next to it, or between it and the range top. We relocated the cooktop closer to the corner, to make room for 18-inch base and wall cabinets between the oven and burner unit.

We installed a food processor base flush with the top of the 18-inch base cabinet. Compartments in the cabinet contain the food processor attachments. We installed an electrical outlet in the wall behind the

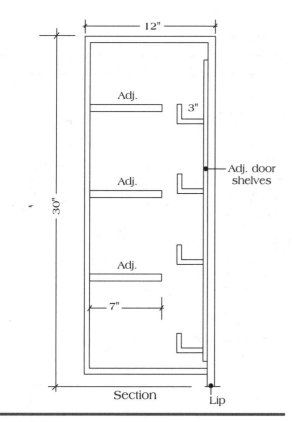

Figure 4-5
Spice cabinet with shelves on the door

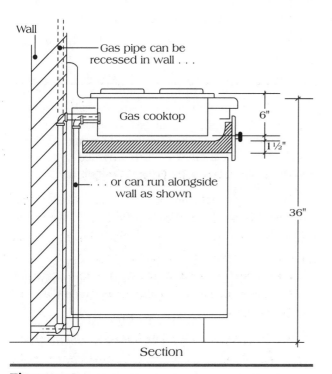

Figure 4-6
Drawer installed under cooktop

base cabinet to plug in the processor, and cut an opening into the cabinet back to access the outlet.

Above the food processor cabinet, we made a spice and condiment cabinet. That cabinet looks just like the other uppers from the outside. But inside, the shelves are set back from the door to allow space for shallow shelves in the door itself. Those door shelves are just the right size to hold one course of spice bottles or cans. All the shelves are adjustable.

Figure 4-5 shows how to design the cabinet. Notice that the cabinet shelves are only 7 inches deep. That's to allow room for the 3-inch shelves on the door.

There are two ways to make the cabinet shelves adjustable. One is to drill holes in the sides of the cabinet to accept metal or plastic seats which support the shelves. The other is to install wall standards available from the hardware store. Those are perforated metal strips which accept seats or brackets at ½-inch intervals. Some better-grade cabinets come with those strips recessed into the cabinet walls.

No matter which system you use, you must be sure the rows of holes or openings in the standards are perfectly even with each other. Otherwise, your shelves won't be level.

The door shelves can rest on brackets inserted into wall standards, or you can buy ready-made plastic units designed to mount inside the cabinet door. These shelves must have a lip on three sides to keep the food containers from falling off the front or sides of the shelves.

A Special Drawer We installed a shallow utensil drawer and two pullout shelves for pots and pans under the electric cooktop. Figure 4-6 shows how you can build a drawer to fit under a gas cooktop. There's less room in this case, because gas units are usually deeper than electric ones, but it can still be done. The drawer face looks just like any other drawer at the top of a base cabinet. But the drawer itself is only 1½ inches deep.

This special drawer is divided into compartments to organize flat objects like knives, spatulas, and other small items. You could also use this space for a cutlery drawer. Those are outfitted with a slotted section where a knife is held upright in each slot. The drawer is often lined with cork or other material which keeps the knives from becoming dull or damaging the drawer as they slide in and out.

A full-sized cutlery drawer can have a sliding cutting board installed over the knife compartment. Both

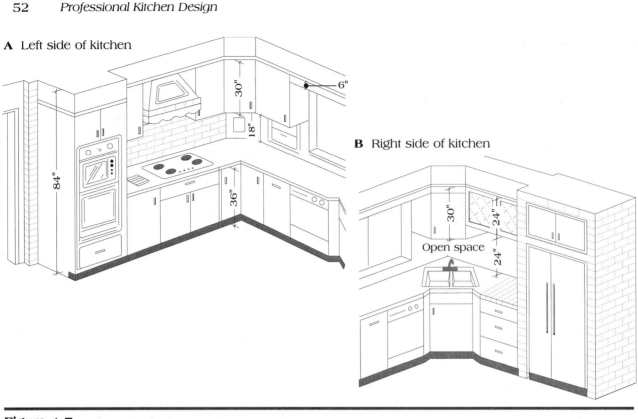

A Left side of kitchen

B Right side of kitchen

Open space

Figure 4-7
Elevations for Figure 4-4

sections are concealed by a false drawer front with spring hinges on its bottom edge. If you're a cabinet-maker and have the necessary tools, you could build this unit yourself. Otherwise, you can order it from your cabinet manufacturer.

There's a full lazy Susan in the corner with a wall cabinet above it. The corner cabinet has a false back that extends to the countertop. The false back keeps things from sliding out of reach on the cabinet shelves. It also provides a place at countertop level for a built-in can opener. There's an electrical outlet on the wall behind the angled wall.

Notice the trash bin between the lazy Susan cabinet and the dishwasher. That space could also be used for a trash compactor, or another drawer base.

The indented corner sink frees up counter space and leaves plenty of room to stand by the open dishwasher. Also, notice that it's easier to reach into the corner cabinet if the sink is indented. The plumbing for the sink was installed at the back of the corner to leave more space under the sink itself. The sink cabinet has a large roll-out shelf to hold detergents and other household chemicals.

Notice that the upper corner cabinet and the cabinet next to it open on both the breakfast room and

kitchen side. The carousel in the corner cabinet is about 17 inches in diameter – large enough that almost anything smaller than a full-sized dinner plate will fit between the rim and the spindle.

Figure 4-7 has the elevation drawings of the plan in Figure 4-4. Notice that the shorter cabinet has glass doors on both the kitchen and breakfast room sides. Since this cabinet is 24 inches high, there's room for a shelf. But you can't put a shelf in a cabinet that's only 18 inches high. A light fixture in the top of the cabinet illuminates the cabinet contents. Where there's room, use a glass shelf in a lighted upper cabinet. The glass should be at least ¼ inch thick, with polished edges.

The drawer cabinet to the right of the sink holds silverware and features a stainless-steel-lined drawer for bread storage. Its metal lining and sliding cover help insulate for moisture. These liners can be made to order for a particular drawer size. The top of the cabinet is covered with a maple cutting board.

The brick refrigerator enclosure adds texture to the design and provides a decorative backdrop for plants and pictures on the breakfast room side.

Once the refrigerator was moved from the end wall, there was room for a 21-inch-wide floor-to-ceil-

C Breakfast room side

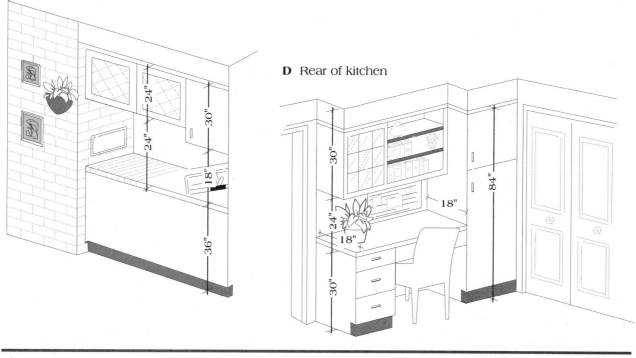

D Rear of kitchen

Figure 4-7 (cont.)
Elevations for Figure 4-4

ing pantry and a desk with a filing cabinet base. All the pantry shelves roll out, and the adjacent desk provides the necessary counter space. We reversed the swing of the double doors so they don't interfere with the pantry.

Shelves over the desk can hold cookbooks, china, or stemware. We installed the telephone and a bulletin board in the space between the shelf unit and the desk top. We also put a concealed light fixture under the upper cabinet.

We've added a brick veneer to the wall behind the range top to match the enclosure for the refrigerator. In Chapter 14, you'll find more information about installing such a wall surface.

An Obstructed U Kitchen

Figure 4-8 shows both plan and elevation view of an already compact U-shaped kitchen that's lost a corner to a water heater enclosure. The flaw is further compounded by poor use of the available space.

Figure 4-9 shows the same kitchen after we applied the Basic Rules and made several other improvements. The new layout improves both the

appearance and function of this kitchen. Starting at the refrigerator and moving clockwise, here's what we did:

First, we took out the little stub wall next to the refrigerator. That added a few inches to the wall space and enough room so the refrigerator door can open fully without obstruction. We extended the cabinet over the refrigerator and installed moveable vertical dividers inside to hold trays, cookie sheets or anything flat.

Next, we built a tall pantry cabinet with pull-out shelves at the end of the refrigerator wall. The remaining base cabinet between the refrigerator and the pantry provides the required counter space. We allowed the soffit to run, uninterrupted, between the refrigerator and the pantry. A light fixture is recessed into this soffit in front of the set-back upper cabinet.

Adding a soffit, upper cabinets and a valance to the window wall tied the two sides of the kitchen together. The upper cabinet to the right of the window is a corner unit with a carousel. We installed a half lazy Susan in the base cabinet beneath it. Finally, we changed the base cabinet beside the range to a drawer unit. You can see that a relatively few, simple changes greatly improved the function of this kitchen.

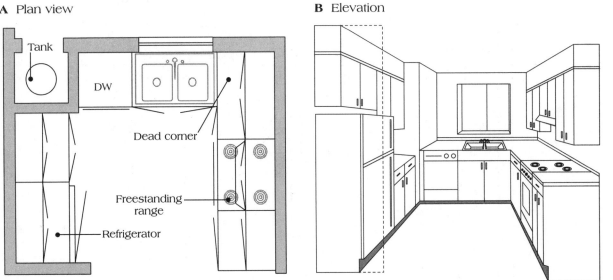

A Plan view

Tank

DW

Dead corner

Freestanding range

Refrigerator

B Elevation

Figure 4-8
A corner is lost in this U kitchen

There's an Alternative to This Layout

In most cases, there's more than one way to improve a bad kitchen arrangement. Figure 4-10 shows another approach to the problems in Figure 4-8.

As you can see, appliances are in the same place as in Figure 4-9, but we've moved the sink to the corner. That allowed us to add both more drawer space and counter surface, although we did sacrifice some shelf space.

In this arrangement, there's drawer space next to the dishwasher, and more counter space between the dishwasher and the sink. We replaced the drawer base to the right of the range with a mini-pantry that opens on the long side. You could also use a conventional base unit here.

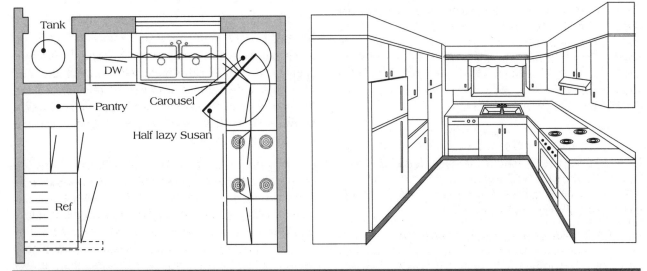

A Plan view

Tank

DW

Pantry

Carousel

Half lazy Susan

Ref

A Elevation

Figure 4-9
A better arrangement comes from changing only the cabinets

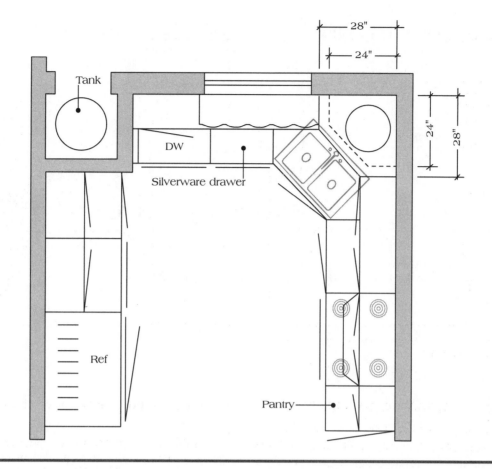

Figure 4-10
An alternate plan required moving the sink

I've shown two sets of measurements for the upper corner cabinet. If you use the larger of the two sizes, you'll have a shorter reach to the front of the upper cabinet when you're standing in front of the sink. If you indent the sink, you won't have as far to reach. But you'll have to be careful not to bump your head if your upper cabinet is only 24 inches above the countertop. Here's a case where your design may depend on your customer's height.

The corner sink arrangement has at least two advantages over our first solution. First, it breaks up the box-like look which kitchens tend to have. Second, it allows a well-lighted, more spacious countertop in front of the window, creating a kitchen any owner (or builder) can be proud of.

This kitchen is only 5½ feet wide between cabinets. A U-shaped kitchen can have as little as 4 feet between cabinets and still be functional. If that distance is greater than 8 feet, it's time to consider a method to break up the space. Otherwise, the cook will waste too many steps moving from one work area to another.

Depending on the amount of space available, and the shape of the room, there are a couple of ways you can solve the problem of too much space. In the next two chapters we'll describe in more detail the use of islands or peninsulas to improve function in a large kitchen. Both these features tie a large kitchen together, and offer work and storage space within easy reach of nearby work stations.

As with any kitchen, the most efficient U kitchen depends on proper placement of the major appliances, and how well you adhere to the Basic Rules for counter space. In a small kitchen, you might not have room for a cooktop and a wall oven – you'd have to use a freestanding range instead. You'd use a top-and-bottom refrigerator instead of a side-by-side. You'd use a lot of common sense, which is 80 percent of the success of any good kitchen design.

Test Questions for Chapter 4

1. Why is the U-shaped kitchen the easiest to design?

2. What are the major design flaws in the kitchen in Figure 4-1?

3. What's the most obvious mistake in the design of the kitchen in Figure 4-3?

4. What benefits did the redesign of the kitchen, as shown in Figure 4-4, achieve?

5. What benefits were gained by removing the non-bearing wall?

6. Why did we install an indented kitty-corner sink in this redesign?

7. Why was the base cabinet placed between the sink and the refrigerator?

8. Why did we reverse the swing of the double doors?

9. Describe a few of the changes that made the kitchen in Figure 4-8 more useful.

10. Would a continuous soffit solve the problem of the empty window wall in Figure 4-8?

CHAPTER 5
The Peninsula Kitchen

The peninsula kitchen is very much like the U-shaped kitchen in both shape and character. But the difference between the two is significant. The U kitchen has three walls; the peninsula has only two, with a counter-high base unit in place of the third wall.

The peninsula offers many advantages. It's most useful when you have a kitchen that's much longer than it is wide. It breaks up the space and puts the kitchen work areas closer together, saving steps for the cook. Whether and how you include a peninsula in your kitchen design depends on your customers' preference and pocketbook, and even on their height.

The peninsula kitchen provides more counter space and more cabinets than an L kitchen. And it offers continuity between the kitchen and adjoining dining area or family room that you can't get with a U kitchen. The peninsula design is especially appropriate for today's trend to provide a feeling of openness in smaller homes.

Once you and the customer have decided on a peninsula kitchen, your first step is to determine how large it can be. Use as much of the available space as possible without crowding the kitchen. Your customer still has to be able to get around it easily.

Next, decide what appliances or fixtures you'll install in the peninsula. If there's going to be a range top, you have to allow for ventilation, either a downdraft unit which exhausts outdoors, or a hood and fan. If you put a sink in the peninsula, you'll have to provide plumbing. And every peninsula needs adequate lighting.

Because a peninsula creates an additional corner, you must design your layout to avoid dead, inaccessible spaces.

How Tall Is Your Client?

Your customer's height may be what determines whether you'll install cabinets above the peninsula or not. If your clients are tall, they may object to the visual barrier. If they're very short, they may be unable to reach the upper cabinets easily.

A Standard height for base and wall cabinets   **B** Standard height for peninsula and upper cabinets   **C** Allow extra space for taller clients

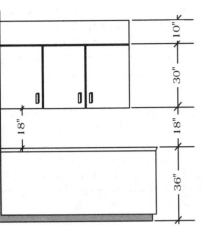
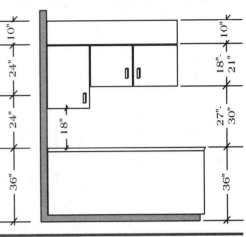

Figure 5-1
Standard spacing between upper and base cabinets

A person of average height can easily see through the opening without stooping if the upper cabinets are 24 inches above the countertop. But a taller person might prefer a space of 27 inches or more. Be sure you're certain about that at the design stage, not after you install the uppers.

Usually, the more space you leave between the upper cabinets and the countertop, the shorter the cabinets will be. The exception would be when there's a cathedral ceiling. Then the upper cabinets can be any height you want. But avoid extremes. Anything too far out of the ordinary could make the house hard to sell later.

In Figure 5-1 you can see three arrangements of upper peninsula cabinets, viewed from outside the kitchen. In most cases, it's handy to have these cabinets open from both sides. Notice that in all three variations, the corner cabinet can drop to within 18 inches of the counter. View A shows the accepted distance between ordinary upper and base cabinets. But avoid this in a pass-through situation. There's not enough clearance between the cabinets.

View B is the normal distance for peninsula cabinets. View C is the option you would probably use for a taller client. Of course, if you don't have a soffit or dropped ceiling, the upper cabinets can be about 10 inches taller.

Soffits or Not?

You'll notice most of my illustrations show soffits. However, there are several options to this treatment. One is to install cabinets all the way to a standard 8-foot ceiling. Where storage space is at a premium, this gives the advantage of an additional shelf in each upper cabinet. Of course, anything stored there can only be reached with a ladder or step stool. And it can make a small room seem unusually tall and cramped.

You could also install a separate bank of cabinets in place of the soffit. Or you can simply leave the space above the cabinets open, to display decorative objects or plants.

Where the kitchen has a vaulted or unusually high ceiling, soffits provide a visual as well as a physical boundary above the cabinets, making the room seem cozier. They serve a similar purpose where walls are normal height, making the room appear wider.

The Range or Cooktop in the Peninsula

In a very small L kitchen, you can gain space and add convenience by building a peninsula to house the range or cooktop. But you may run into a problem if the peninsula is very short. The cooktop might be flush with the internal corner, as in Figure 5-2. In that case, one way you can use the resulting dead corner is to provide access from the room outside the peninsula. You could also install a lazy Susan if there's space on the adjacent wall.

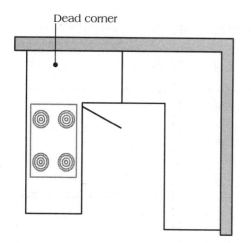

Dead corner

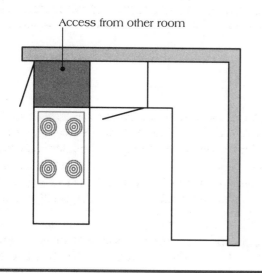

Access from other room

Figure 5-2
Access to dead corner from outside the peninsula

Venting a Range or Cooktop in a Peninsula

There are two ways to vent a range or cooktop in a peninsula. The same methods apply for an island. In the first method, fumes are drawn down by an exhaust fan into the top or top rear of the cooking unit. In the second method, you install an exhaust fan in a hood over the range or cooktop.

Overhead exhaust fans for island or peninsula ranges must be more powerful than those for a range that stands against a wall. There are two reasons for this. First, there's a greater volume of air to be circulated, and second, the fan must be powerful enough to offset drafts created when doors or windows are open elsewhere in the room.

Exhaust power is measured in cubic feet of air exchanged per minute, or CFM. For a range installed against a wall, use a fan that's equal in rating to 100 CFM per linear foot of vent hood. A fan in a hood over an island or peninsula should provide 120 CFM for each linear foot of hood.

Using those guidelines, you can mount a hood not less than 21 inches, but not more than 30 inches, above a cooktop. When the distance is greater than 30 inches, other factors such as total room size must be considered. See Chapter 10 for more detailed information about capacities and requirements for exhaust systems.

The vent hood over a peninsula is usually flared on the kitchen side, but flush with any accompanying cabinets on the back side. That's illustrated in Figure 5-3. The exhaust duct takes up part of the space in the cabinet above the vent hood. There isn't anything you

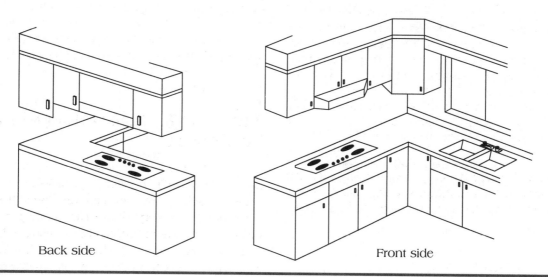

Back side   Front side

Figure 5-3
Range hood is flared on kitchen side, flat on back

A Peninsula with a 36-inch exhaust fan   **B** Peninsula with a 30-inch exhaust fan

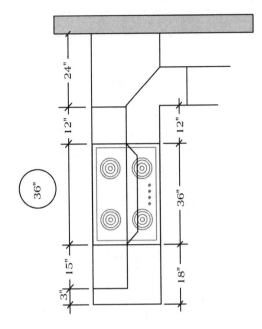   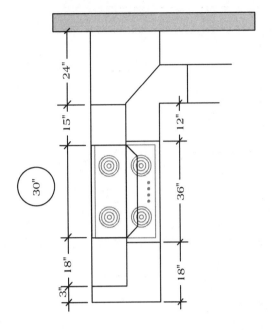

Figure 5-4
You can use a 30-inch hood over a 36-inch range

can do about that. But you can often adjust the size of cabinets on either side of the hood.

Figure 5-4 shows a small 66-inch peninsula with a 36-inch cooktop. You can see that the uppers are the same size as the bases, except for the end one. That's because upper cabinets must be recessed at least 3 inches from the end of the peninsula to prevent head injury when a person steps close to the base cabinet. On the front of an upper-base combination, the uppers must be set back at least 9 inches, but 12 inches is better.

Notice that one of the upper cabinets in View A is only 12 inches wide. Some people might consider that too narrow to be practical. There are a couple of ways you can fix that without making the peninsula any longer. The first is to use a 30-inch hood over the 36-inch range. That allows the cabinets on both sides of the hood to be 3 inches wider. This method doesn't reduce the effectiveness of the vent hood, as long as the fan is the proper capacity for the situation. Figure 5-4 B shows that solution.

The other way is to use a 30-inch hood and range, as shown in Figure 5-5 A. But if you install the range flush with the corner cabinet, you can see the sizes of the cabinets beside the hood will be very different.

Solve that by separating the range from the return cabinet at the corner with a 4-inch filler, as shown in Figure 5-5 B. Then the uppers will be a more useful size.

If you don't install cabinets over a peninsula, you'd use the same kind of vent as for an island cooktop. But there's one problem you have to watch out for in a peninsula kitchen.

You may occasionally want to install the range or cooktop immediately next to a corner base which has an upper associated with it. In that case, you must be sure the range hood doesn't prevent the cabinet door from opening. The hood can flare toward the front, but not on the sides. And the cabinet door should open on the side away from the vent hood. You could also use horizontal tambour doors in the cabinet.

You could also recess the exhaust fan into the cabinet. In this case, you'd need a fan with a higher CFM rating to compensate for the distance from the cooking surface. Fortunately, today's exhaust systems come with quieter, more powerful fans than ever before. As a designer, you have plenty of flexibility, and the technology to back you up. We cover exhaust systems in more detail in Chapter 10.

A Peninsula with a 30-inch range and exhaust fan

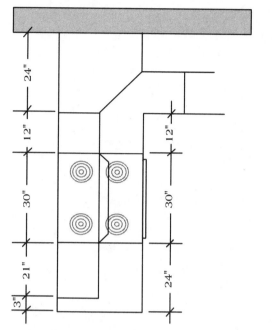

B Peninsula with the range centered to equalize cabinet sizes

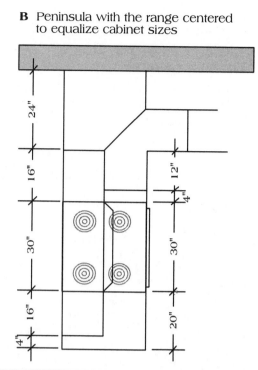

Figure 5-5
Use a filler to center a 30-inch range under the upper cabinets

Sinks in Peninsulas

When you locate a sink in a peninsula, don't place it at the end. Leave room for a cabinet between the sink cabinet and the end of the peninsula. The end cabinet can be either a shelf or drawer base. And it's always handy to have a towel drawer near the sink.

When you install a sink in a peninsula or island, you have to alter the kitchen's plumbing. Figure 5-6 A shows how you'd provide drainage where there's a crawl space, another room, or a basement under the floor. Figure 5-6 B shows how to route the drain above the slab. (In the case of an island installation, you'd have to drill a channel in the slab to contain the drain.)

If the distance to the stack is more than 5 feet, increase the drain line from 2 inches to up to 4 inches, properly pitched to drain. Figure 5-7 is a chart showing the maximum distance from trap to vent for trap arms of different sizes.

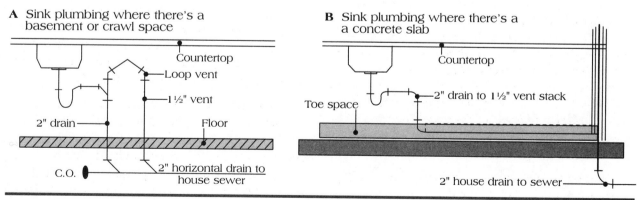

Figure 5-6
Drainage plumbing in a peninsula

Trap arm size	Max. distance, trap to vent
1¼"	2'6"
1½"	3'6"
2"	5'
3"	6'
4"	10'

Figure 5-7
Maximum distance from trap to vent

Small Appliances in Peninsulas

The peninsula is a convenient location for built-in blender or food processor bases. These don't clutter up the counter space when they're not in use, and the peninsula cabinets are a handy place to store the components. Avoid putting these appliances at the end of the peninsula. Like the sink or cooktop, these machines are most useful when they have plenty of counter space on both sides of them.

It's best to install these appliances in a perfectly flat surface such as wood, plastic laminate, stainless steel, marble, or Corian. Don't put them on tile, especially rustic tile that has an uneven surface. The grout spaces will be a nuisance to keep clean.

Glass Doors on Peninsula Cabinets

Solid cabinets over a peninsula form a visual barrier that detracts from the open look between two areas. One way to minimize the barrier is to use clear, stained, or colored glass for the doors. You can further add to the open look by using glass shelves if the cabinet will be used to store crystal, stemware, or other transparent items. It's an especially nice, and inexpensive, touch to install light fixtures in the top of the cabinets. The light will filter through and around the cabinets. This treatment is both decorative and practical.

You can tap off the existing ceiling light circuit, providing the power goes to the ceiling box first, then to the wall switch. If the line goes to the switch first, you'll have to tap off the junction box which gets its power from the ceiling light box. Power then goes from the panel to the ceiling box, then returns to the panel.

Wire switches for all the fixtures from the new junction box. The under-counter fixtures are self-switched and easy to reach. Mount the switch for the lights in the top of the upper peninsula cabinet on the side or bottom of the cabinet itself.

Check with your local building inspector or refer to the electrical code to be sure you don't install too many fixtures on each circuit. Add circuits to the existing panel box if you can, or install a larger or additional panel.

The under-cabinet fluorescent lights produce little heat, so no special ventilation is required. They're self-switched, and connected to a new or existing lighting circuit. Don't wire them from an existing wall outlet or switch.

The Peninsula As Seating Space

If there's room, you'll often be asked to include seating space along a peninsula. There's a potential design flaw in this situation that's often overlooked. Avoid having more than two people sitting in a straight line if you can. The ones on the ends can't see past those in the middle. See Figure 5-8 A.

Allow a minimum of 6 inches beside a chair or stool for each person who will be seated around a table or snack bar. That means allow 24 inches for each chair if the chairs are 18 inches wide, and 30 inches for chairs which are 24 inches wide.

If the snack bar or breakfast bar is large enough for four or more people, curve it so the people on the ends can see each other. Figure 5-8 B shows an example. Allow an overhang or depth of at least 12 inches for a snack bar.

When possible, place the snack bar at table height (28-30 inches) rather than countertop height. That way you can use chairs instead of stools. Chairs are easier to maneuver, and they're more convenient to use for extra seating when company comes. Many people aren't comfortable sitting on a bar stool in the middle of the room, even when the stool has its own footrest.

When a snack bar is at countertop height, always make it part of the countertop itself. Never attach it separately. When you attach a table-high surface to a standard 36-inch-high base cabinet, use corbels or

A Avoid three chairs in a straight line

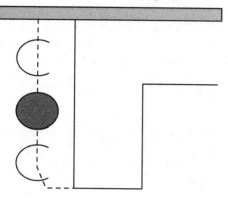

B Provide a curved bar for three or more people

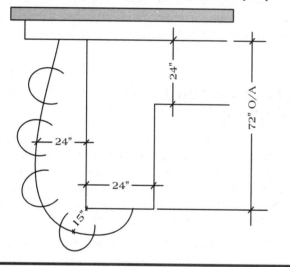

Figure 5-8
Curve a snack bar for three or more people

decorative brackets to support the snack bar. Be sure the cabinet wall is at least ¾ inch thick to hold the screws without letting them penetrate the cabinet wall.

To fasten a wooden leg to a snack bar or desk, cut a 4 x 4 inch piece of wood from ¾-inch-thick stock. Bevel the edges for a finished look. Then fasten this block to the top of the leg with glue and a countersunk screw. Drill pilot holes near the four corners of the wood block, and screw it into the underside of the desk or tabletop.

You can also use manufactured legs which come with a mounting plate attached. Be sure the mounting screws you use don't penetrate the top of the article you're supporting.

Wall-Mounted Furniture

There are several ways you can install a wall-mounted desk top. One is to build the desk drawer housing with a top, back, sides, and front. You can add a bottom panel after the unit is installed. Use corner braces at the back of the unit to keep it square. Drive screws through the back of the drawer housing and into the studs of the wall behind it. The drawer can ride on a center glide, or in runners attached to the sides of the desk itself.

Another method is to extend the back of the drawer unit all the way to the floor. Then you can screw the back to the studs in several places. Figure 5-9 illustrates these two methods.

A third way is to include a support as part of the drawer unit's side, and screw the opposite side into the adjoining cabinet.

A Full ¾" back as part of desk (front view)

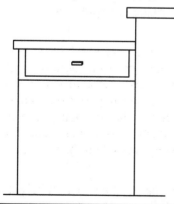

B One-piece side support part of desk (side view)

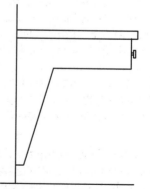

Figure 5-9
How to support a wall-mounted desk

The Ideal Peninsula Kitchen

The peninsula is used most effectively where the kitchen/eating area is long and narrow, where a full wall is too confining, and a half wall adds nothing to the area's usefulness. A peninsula gives the storage and step-saving advantages of an enclosure without sacrificing spaciousness. We've seen that it can also serve as extra seating space.

It's possible to design a functional peninsula kitchen in a space as small as 7 feet wide, as you can see in Figure 5-10. It's not recommended, because it's best to leave at least 4 feet of open floor space between cabinets. But you can get away with it if the kitchen is built for a single user.

When the space between the peninsula and its opposite wall exceeds 8 feet, it's time to consider breaking up the space. Either move the peninsula, or add an island.

The Peninsula As a Remodeling Tool

In Figure 5-11 you can see a tiny, cramped, inefficient kitchen. Two simple structural changes let us make this kitchen functional and attractive. First, we took out the wall between the kitchen and family room. This wasn't a loadbearing wall, so removing it was a simple job. Had it been loadbearing, we would have had to brace it as described on page 66.

Figure 5-12 shows the new design. First, we moved the window to the left to make room for the kitty-corner cabinet to the right of the sink. Then we built a new peninsula that extends 7 inches farther into the family room, beyond the location of the original wall. The peninsula houses the freestanding range, with cabinets and the range hood over the peninsula.

The upper cabinets between the range and the sink open on both the kitchen and the family room

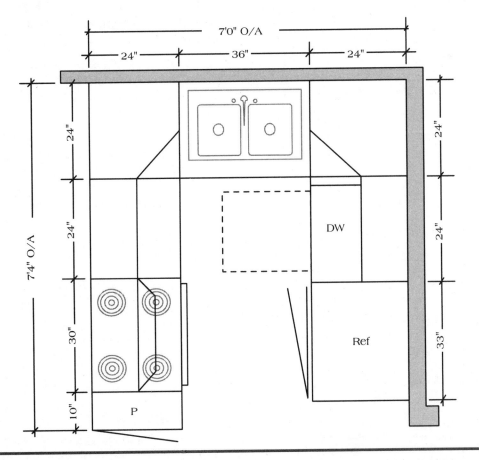

Figure 5-10

A peninsula kitchen in as little as 7 feet

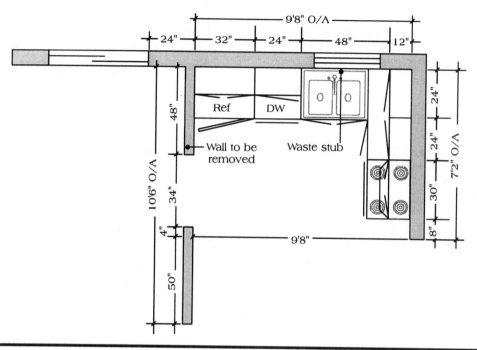

Figure 5-11
A crowded kitchen with room to grow

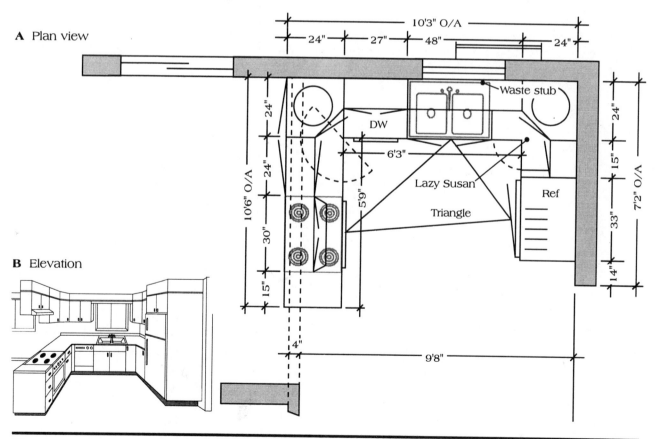

Figure 5-12
A peninsula with cabinets above makes this kitchen work

sides. And we installed lazy Susans in both base corners. Notice that there's no upper cabinet between the range hood and the end of the peninsula. That's because there wasn't enough room for a useful cabinet, once we allowed for the required setback. You can see that even with slightly less floor space, this kitchen has at least twice the convenience.

When You Remove a Bearing Wall

When ceiling joists are supported separately on both sides of a loadbearing wall, you can use a method called fishplating to make the beams self-supporting. You could use 1-inch-thick wood cleats for this purpose, but it's best to use ¼-inch steel plates securely bolted as shown in Figure 5-13. The cleats or plates must be the same height as the beams they're reinforcing, and not less than 24 inches long.

Erect temporary supporting frames on both sides of the wall you're removing, and leave them in place until the job of reinforcing the joists is complete. Install the supports about 3 feet from the existing wall so you'll have room to work. Use 2 x 4s for the support uprights and space them on 24-inch centers. Make the temporary support ½ inch to 1 inch shorter than the room height and pad the top to protect the

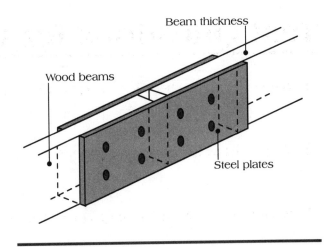

Figure 5-13
Fishplating supports separate joists

ceiling. Now you can tip the supporting frame into place without hitting the ceiling. Then shim it from the bottom so it fits tightly.

In the next chapter, we'll discuss a similar situation, the island kitchen. We'll show how an island ties together a kitchen that's so large that the occupant has to walk too far between work areas on more than two sides. The peninsula works best to break up a long, narrow kitchen, but an island adds convenience to a large room of any shape.

Test Questions for Chapter 5

1. Name at least two benefits that a peninsula kitchen provides.

2. Why is the height of your client important in this type of kitchen?

3. What is the normal distance between a peninsula counter and the cabinets above it?

4. Explain two ways of venting a cooking appliance on a peninsula.

5. What is the standard way of measuring the capacity of a fan?

6. Why is it necessary to set back the upper cabinet at the end of a peninsula?

7. Name two ways to run the 2-inch drain from the sink on a peninsula.

8. When installing a built-in blender or food-processor base, what kind of surface should you choose for the countertop?

9. What are two advantages of using clear or stained-glass doors on upper peninsula cabinets?

10. What's the minimum kitchen width in which you can build a functional peninsula?

CHAPTER 6
The Island Kitchen

My guess is that fewer than 2 percent of all the homes in America have island cabinets. They're very rare in older homes (built before 1950) and aren't common even in modern tract homes. So why devote an entire chapter to the island kitchen? Easy. Just open any home design magazine. What do you see? Miles and miles of island cabinets and island kitchens.

People planning to spend thousands remodeling a kitchen want what's in style, what their kitchen doesn't have now, and, of course, what they see in home design magazines. Maybe that's why so many remodeled kitchens become island kitchens. If you're in the kitchen design and remodeling business, you'd better also be in the island kitchen business.

It's easy to make mistakes when you plan an island kitchen. Ignore a few simple rules and you'll create a kitchen that's neither attractive nor functional. It doesn't cost much more to do it right. Understand the examples in this chapter and you'll avoid the most common pitfalls. You'll also recognize situations where an island kitchen is a good choice both for the home and for the owners.

When should you recommend an island layout? Suggest a center island any time a kitchen has a center open space of 8 feet or more. Besides providing a step-saving work surface, an island adds storage space. A useful island can be as small as 24 inches square. But allow a minimum of 3 feet of open space all around the island – 42 inches is better.

Figure 6-1 shows a typical 3- by 6-foot island cabinet. It's counter high (36 inches), and the base cabinet storage space is 24 inches deep. Knee space under an island snack bar like this can be as little as 8 inches.

Island cabinets add convenience to a large kitchen. You can install a full-sized sink or bar sink, cooktop, grill, rotisserie, or appliance base in the top. Just don't install any of these on the ends of the island where there won't be counter space on both sides. Cabinets can have stationary or sliding shelves, drawers, or bins. The doors can swing or slide. Counter height should be 36 inches (for stools) or 28 to 30 inches high for table seating.

If you're gutting an existing kitchen, or planning one from scratch, here's how to lay out your design for a functional island kitchen.

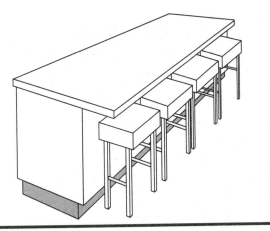

Figure 6-1
An island makes room for base cabinets and seating

First, measure the available space. You need at least 12 feet for an island, so there's room for a 3-foot aisle between a 24-inch island and any surrounding cabinets.

Next, determine what the exposure to the outdoors will be. Place the window over the sink, or by the breakfast bar, where you can take best advantage of a lovely view. Will the room be subject to direct sunshine? Then don't arrange the room so that people can't eat by the window or work by the sink at mealtimes because of the heat or glare.

Now, lay out the floor plan. Follow the five Basic Rules and keep the work triangle within 21 feet overall. Avoid letting the island interfere with any leg of the triangle. If the island will house a sink, range or cooktop, decide how to route the utilities or plumbing. If you're doing a remodel, you may have to cut the concrete slab, move doors and windows, and beef up the electrical service. Take plenty of time to plan the job carefully. Time spent on planning will pay off later on.

A Small Kitchen in a Big Room

Figure 6-2 is a poorly-designed kitchen that, at 13 by 17 feet, has plenty of room for a center island. But lots of that space is wasted.

We made two structural changes in this kitchen. First, we moved the recessed window flush with the outside wall. Then we extended the refrigerator wall 3 feet. The rest of the changes were a simple matter of adding new cabinets. The original appliances and fixtures were fine.

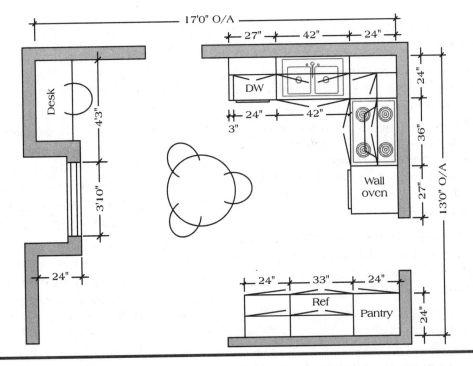

Figure 6-2
There's lots of wasted space in this bad kitchen design

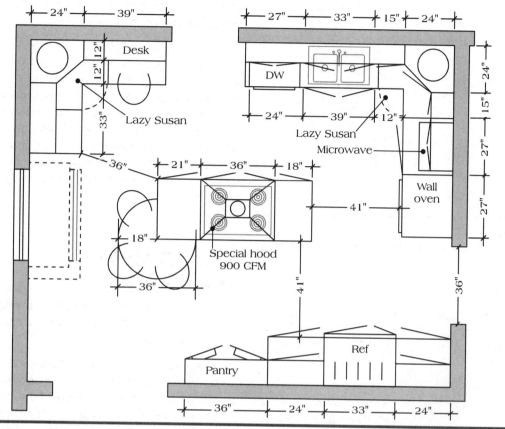

Figure 6-3
New design uses space efficiently

Notice in Figure 6-2 that the cooktop is at a right angle to the sink. That's always an inconvenient layout.

Figure 6-3 is the revised floor plan. Figure 6-4 shows elevations. View A is the sink end of the new kitchen. We moved the dishwasher and sink 12 inches closer to the doorway and installed the cooktop in the island. That made room for a lazy Susan in what had been a useless corner. We made the cabinet over the sink 6 inches narrower than the sink cabinet itself. If we hadn't, the upper cabinet to the right of the sink would have been only 12 inches wide.

We left the wall oven pretty much where it was originally. But now there's room for counter space, an upper cabinet and a suspended microwave next to the wall oven where the cooktop was before.

View B is the center island. The island snack bar is like a pie with a quarter wedge cut out. The counter is table height, 6 inches lower than the main part of the island. If it were countertop height, the best treatment would be a seamless top that covered both the

island and the snack bar. That top would have to be cut from a large piece of stock and would leave a lot of waste. Making the island and snack bar different heights solves this problem.

To attach a snack bar like this one, build it with a ¾-inch-thick lip at least 3 inches deep. Be sure the cabinet walls you'll attach to are also at least ¾ inch thick. Screw through the lip, into the cabinet wall as shown in Figure 6-5. If the snack bar overhang is more than 16 to 18 inches, support it with a bracket or leg.

View C in Figure 6-4 is the refrigerator wall. The extension of the wall behind the refrigerator into the doorway made room for a 12- by 36-inch pantry to replace the floor-to-ceiling cabinet that was 24 inches square. The new pantry takes up less floor space, but has more room for storage than the old one did. That's because the old cabinet had only four stationary shelves, while the new one has eight adjustable ones, plus shallow storage bins in the doors. There's also counter space on both sides of the refrigerator now.

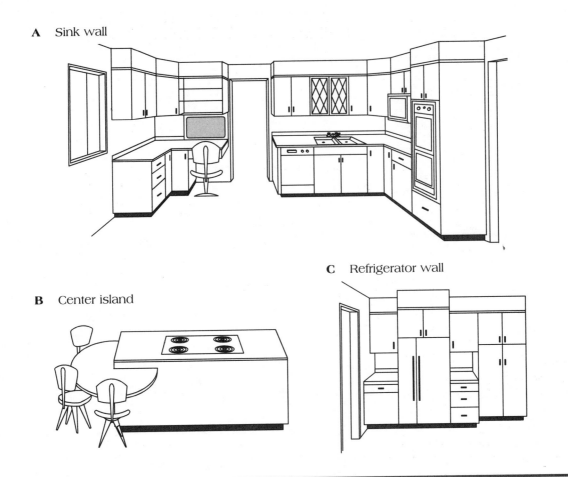

A Sink wall

B Center island

C Refrigerator wall

Figure 6-4
Elevations for Figure 6-3

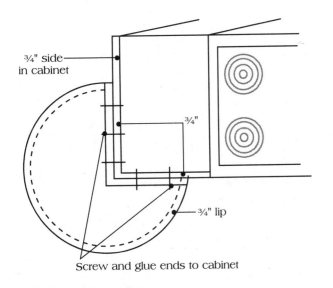

¾" side
in cabinet

¾"

¾" lip

Screw and glue ends to cabinet

Figure 6-5
Attaching a snack bar to an island

Replace a Peninsula with an Island

Figure 6-6 illustrates one of the worst kitchen designs I've ever seen. The peninsula divided this narrow kitchen from the buffet cabinets almost as effectively as a solid wall would have. The wall cabinets over the peninsula base were only 18 inches above the counter. The buffet cabinets had sliding doors, so you could only get into one side at a time. There wasn't enough room to stand between the open oven door and the refrigerator, and there was no room to open the refrigerator door all the way. It was a mess.

The first thing we did was to change the window arrangement. Figure 6-7 shows the floor plan of the remodeled kitchen. We replaced the existing two windows with a single 4-foot window centered over the sink.

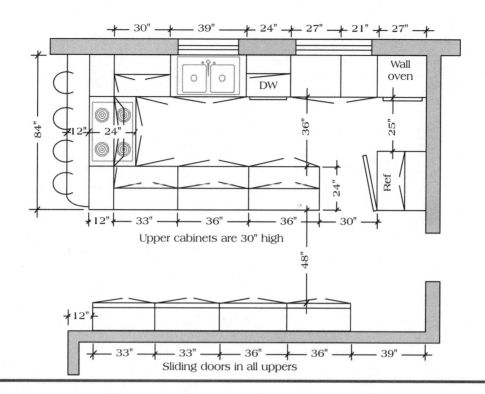

Upper cabinets are 30" high

Sliding doors in all uppers

Figure 6-6

Look for space outside to enlarge a kitchen

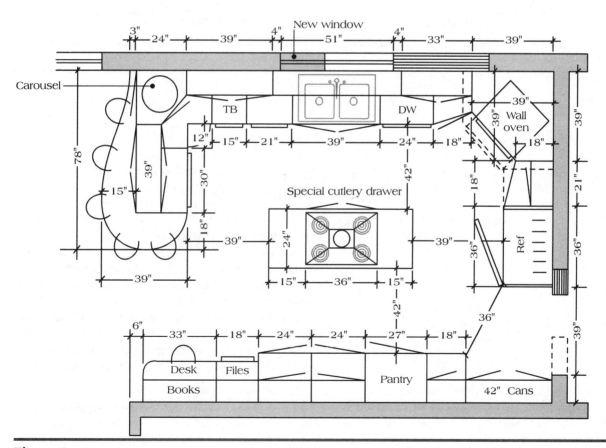

Figure 6-7

The new kitchen is spacious and functional

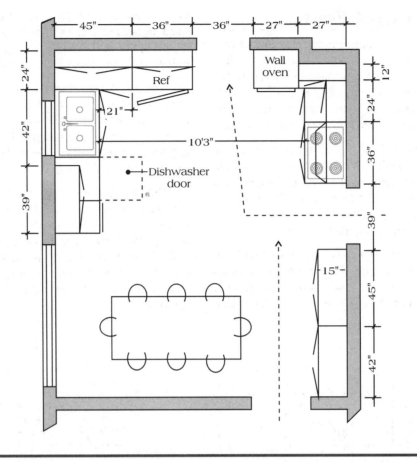

Figure 6-8
This kitchen has its cooktop in the wrong place

Notice the angled base cabinets by the wall oven. You have to order those custom-made, but they're worth the trouble. We set the wall oven into the corner and indented it 6 inches from the base cabinet faces. That gave us an extra 3 inches of width for the base and upper cabinets on both sides of the oven. It also makes it easier to reach the back of the cabinets next to the oven. The dotted lines on Figure 6-7 show how this works.

We shifted the doorway to make more room for the refrigerator. The small stub of wall left enough room for the 12-inch-deep canned goods cabinet. This kitchen now has plenty of cabinet and drawer space, and they're in all the right places. There's a large dish cabinet over the dishwasher. Silverware drawers are convenient to both the dishwasher and the breakfast bar. And the cabinets over the bar open from both sides. There's a deep drawer for kitchen linens near the sink. The trash bin is also conveniently located near the sink. The pantry wall has a desk, file drawers, and cookbook storage.

Adding an Island in a Smaller Kitchen

The range top in Figure 6-8 presents two problems. First, it's next to the doorway, which is dangerous. Second, it's over 10 feet from the sink and that path crosses a traffic pattern. It's best to keep the distance between the cooktop and sink to 6 feet or less, where people won't be crossing the path. An island cooktop seems to be the solution here, but the total floor space wasn't enough for conventional placement of an island. If it were parallel to the sink wall, it would leave too little space at the refrigerator and the table. If it were parallel to the table, it would leave too little space to open the dishwasher door.

Our remedy here took a little imagination, even daring. You can see in Figure 6-9 that by placing the island at a precise angle and easing off the corners, there's enough clearance all the way around. Notice also that we blanked out the dead corner in the upper cabinet by the wall oven.

Big Isn't Always Best

Island kitchens take more space. That places limits on where island cabinets can be used. But sometimes the problem is too much space in a kitchen. It's not easy to design an efficient work triangle in a very large kitchen. You have to be especially careful to tie the major appliances together and avoid wasted steps.

The most noticeable flaw in Figure 6-10 is the location of the dishwasher. As you can see, it's a long walk from the dishwasher to the sink or nearest dish cabinet (marked DC on the plan view). Believe it or not, this arrangement appeared on the cover of a popular home improvement magazine.

Several of the Basic Rules were overlooked here. There are no counters beside the pantries. There's no counter by the refrigerator, and there's not enough counter space around the cooktop or grill. The desk

chair is going to obstruct the doorway and the desk itself is hemmed in by the broom closet. And there are no upper cabinets over the peninsula base – so it extends into the room like an open ironing board.

The most significant change in our redesigned kitchen (Figure 6-11) is placement of the wall oven. Notice that we moved the wall oven to the corner and recessed it from the cabinet faces. The next most important change was to move the dishwasher next to the sink, where it belongs.

We also tore out the pantry and closet walls. Now we could move the refrigerator to the end of the wall, leaving room for the cooktop and plenty of counter space. Once we moved the cooktop to the refrigerator wall, the barbecue grill fit in the middle of the island, providing counter space to both left and right. The desk wall is now unobstructed, with the chair out of the doorway.

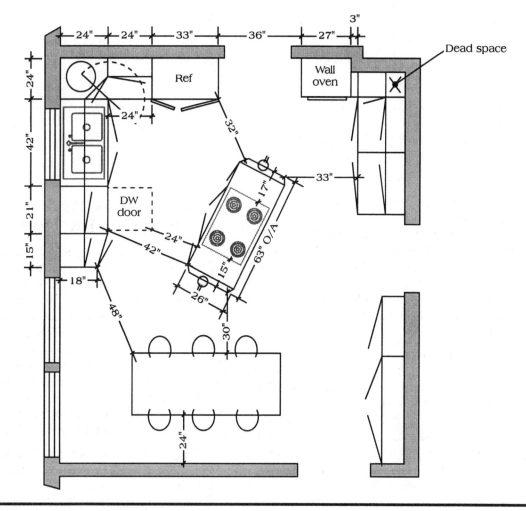

Figure 6-9
An unusual island placement solved the problem

A   Plan view

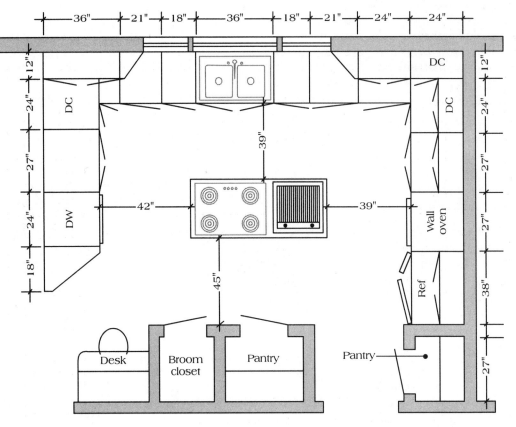

B   Elevation

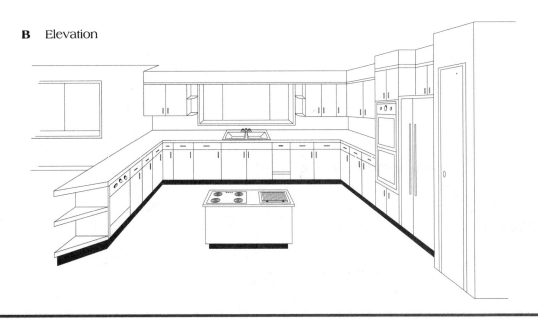

Figure 6-10
The designer of this large kitchen ignored the Basic Rules

A Plan view

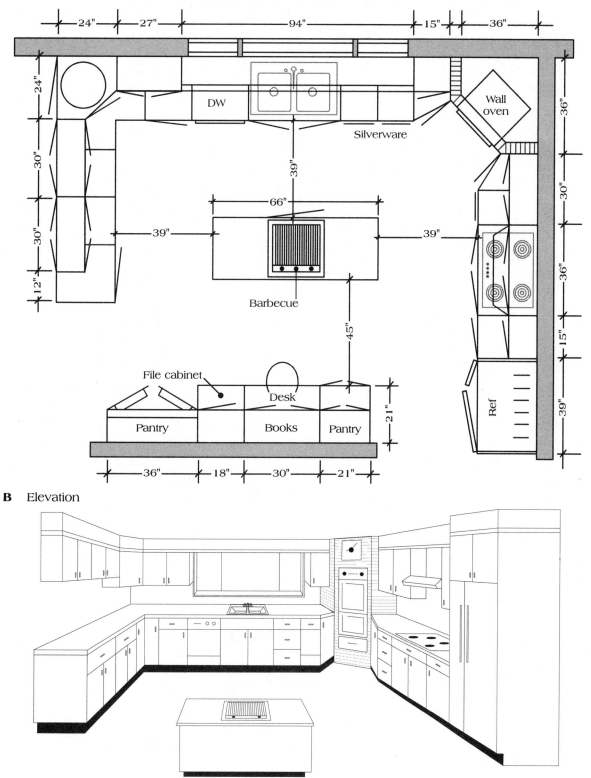

B Elevation

Figure 6-11
The new design is functional and attractive

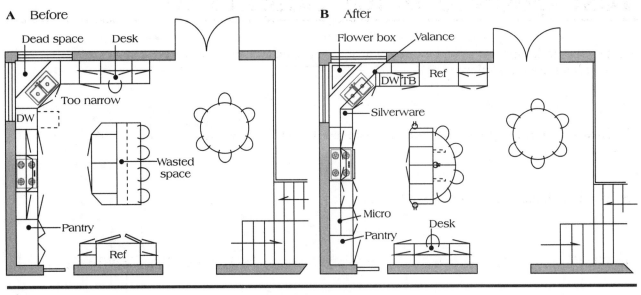

Figure 6-12
One final example

Pay Attention to Traffic

Figure 6-12 A shows a spacious but poorly-designed kitchen. Notice how little space there is in front of the sink when the dishwasher door is open. From our earlier discussion, you know that putting a filler strip between the dishwasher and the sink cabinet adds the work space needed at the sink.

The refrigerator was too far from the sink, requiring a detour around the island to get from the sink to the refrigerator. And the refrigerator is so close to the island that there's no room for passage when the refrigerator door is open.

The large pantry cabinet had only four stationary shelves, each 24 inches deep. That's too deep for stationary shelves in a pantry. It was very hard to reach anything at the back of those shelves. We cut the pantry width to 24 inches, added more shelves and mounted them on glides so they roll out. We provided just as much storage in only half the wall space. There's wasted space in the original island, too.

There's no cooktop, so it's not necessary to allow the extra space for those seated at the counter to be safe from hot splatters.

Figure 6-12 B shows the new design. We added new cabinets at the formerly blank wall next to the double doors. The dishwasher is now on the opposite side of the sink and separated from it by a filler strip to allow more standing room. There's an extra set of cabinets beside the cooktop. The desk is away from the main work area. The refrigerator is close to the sink. We installed a planter box behind the sink and tied the whole corner together with a valance. The new kitchen is roomy, attractive, and efficient.

An island like this one, which doesn't house a sink or cooktop, can be covered in the same material as the rest of the countertops. You can also install a chopping block or a marble pastry board since the island cabinets would be a good place to store a blender, mixer or food processor. In fact, the entire island can have a chopping block top.

Test Questions for Chapter 6

1. On a remodel job, what is the minimum amount of open space a kitchen must have for an island to be installed?

2. How much open space must there be around all sides of an island?

3. What appliance can you place at the end of an island?

4. What's the correct counter height for an island if the seating is stools? What is it for chairs?

5. What are the major design flaws in the kitchen in Figure 6-2?

6. What design change would improve the refrigerator wall in Figure 6-4 C?

7. Name three design flaws in the kitchen in Figure 6-6.

8. In Figure 6-10 A, why is the dishwasher location unworkable?

9. In the kitchen in Figure 6-10 A, the designer built a peninsula with no cabinets above, probably to create an unobstructed view into the other room. Was this the best design for the situation?

10. Why was the dishwasher moved to the right of the sink in the kitchen in Figure 6-12?

CHAPTER 7
Unusual Kitchen Layouts

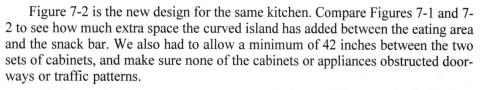

Kitchens aren't always square or rectangular. Some have walls that curve or meet at odd angles. Some have cabinets with irregular shapes. You may be asked to remodel a kitchen like this, or perhaps you'll design one from scratch. In either case, you have to pay special attention to the Basic Rules so these kitchens remain functional.

Figure 7-1 is the plan view of a large kitchen-breakfast area separated by a peninsula. The owner found the layout of this kitchen inconvenient and confining. We solved the problem by rearranging the sink wall and an island into concentric curves.

Figure 7-2 is the new design for the same kitchen. Compare Figures 7-1 and 7-2 to see how much extra space the curved island has added between the eating area and the snack bar. We also had to allow a minimum of 42 inches between the two sets of cabinets, and make sure none of the cabinets or appliances obstructed doorways or traffic patterns.

In redesigning the kitchen, we first decided on the layout for the cabinets along the garage wall and framed a stud wall to mount them on. To reduce costs, the sink unit was left at 24 inches deep for its entire length, but the ends of the curve are 54 inches from the garage wall. Notice that the cabinets are set back about a foot from the garage door jamb. This provides extra clearance, and also room to install the three-way light switches on that wall. There's another three-way light switch at the entry.

We moved the side-by-side refrigerator/freezer to the opposite end of the sink wall so there's a countertop opposite the refrigerator door. We extended the cabinet above the refrigerator and outfitted it for tray storage, and added a wine rack and small cabinet next to the refrigerator. We also replaced the three-bowl sink unit with an offset two-bowl unit that includes a sink big enough to hold large utensils for filling and washing. There's a built-in food processor near the sink. We moved the compactor away from the sink and put a drawer base for silverware and linens in its place.

The space behind the curved main wall now holds a pantry cabinet with roll-out shelves. We closed off the existing pantry on the kitchen side and opened it to the garage instead. By lining the closet wall with 2-inch cinder block and ½-inch

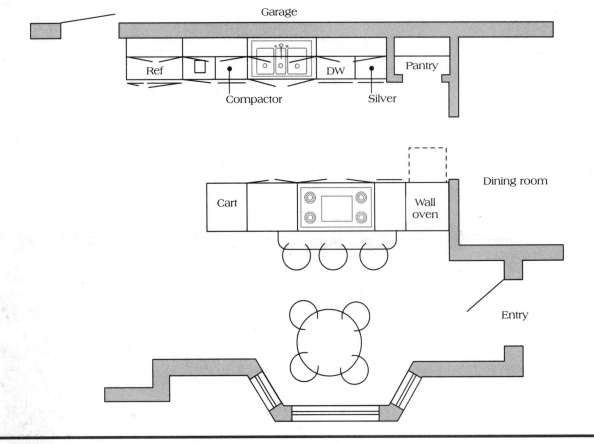

Figure 7-1
A large kitchen with inconvenient traffic flow

drywall, we retained the required fire resistance in the wall between the garage and the house.

The original peninsula is now an island, so there's room to walk from the entry door to the main kitchen wall or the dining room without going all the way around. We used standard cabinets throughout, and installed finish panels on the ones in the island that were exposed from the back. Where the cabinets meet on the inside of a curve, we scribed them flush to one another. At the outside of the curve, we inserted beveled panels to fill the gaps.

The original snack bar put users dangerously close to the range top, so we made it deeper and curved it so people at the ends can see each other. We put a large decorative hood over the cooktop in the island and a counter saver between the range top and the wall oven. The hood contains a powerful 550 CFM fan to draw out smoke and cooking fumes. The wall surrounding the oven unit has a toaster built into it above the counter and snack bar.

The cabinet with the butcher-block top at the end of the island is a rolling cart that can move between the pantry, buffet cabinet and dining room. It's designed for access from both sides with a drawer at the top and an adjustable shelf inside. If you build a cart like this and you want to also use it as a work surface, install locking casters so it only rolls when you want it to. But before you decide to add a rolling cart, first consider the floor surface. It will roll easily on sheet vinyl or wood, but not on Spanish tile or flagstone. Don't include a cart if it's not safe and easy to use.

We built a coat closet next to the entry door, and a buffet on the opposite side of the bay window. Next to the buffet, there's a corner desk with bookshelves above it, file drawers, a bulletin board, and space for a computer.

Supporting the Brick Work

This house is built on a slab, so we didn't have to provide a foundation for the brick oven wall and

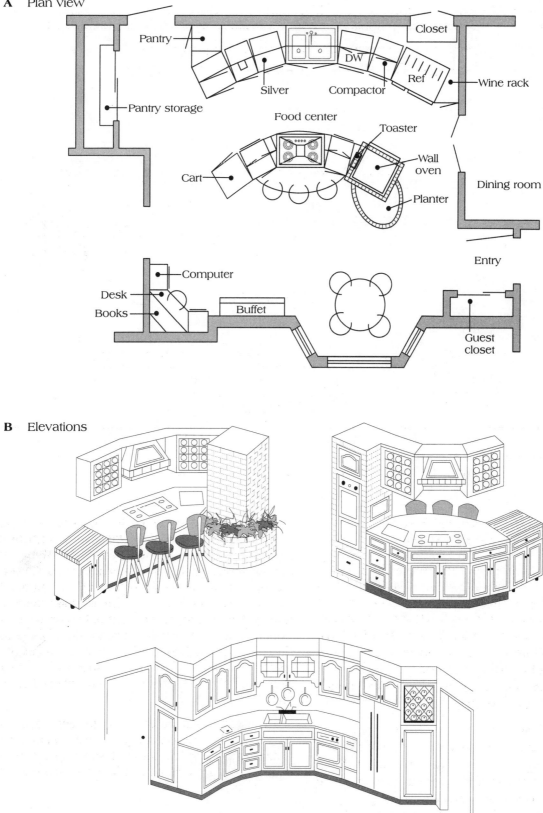

A Plan view

Pantry

Pantry storage

Silver

Compactor

DW

Ref

Closet

Wine rack

Food center

Toaster

Wall oven

Cart

Planter

Dining room

Entry

Computer

Desk

Books

Buffet

Guest closet

B Elevations

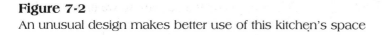

Figure 7-2
An unusual design makes better use of this kitchen's space

A   Plan view

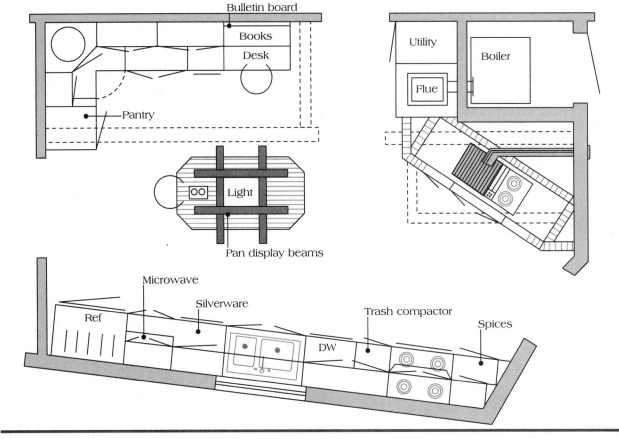

Figure 7-3
A layout designed to show off the brick-enclosed wall

planter. But if you add brick over a basement or crawl space, you'd probably have to reinforce the floor joists to accept the extra load. Chapter 14 has more information on using brick in your kitchen designs. If you want to use live plants in a planter like this, install a floor drain and a pipe chase beneath the floor so water drains outside the building.

We used some imagination to make this kitchen attractive and functional. Our next example also required imaginative solutions, and it incorporated some practical aesthetic features as well.

Design for Visual Impact

Figure 7-3 A is the plan view of a kitchen we designed with a brick archway enclosing an indoor grill. It was important to the owner that the brickwork be visible from the breakfast room off the opposite end of the kitchen.

Before we began this project, the kitchen was long and narrow, with walls that projected awkwardly into the room. The dotted lines on this drawing show where the original walls were located. You can see this kitchen is really a one-wall kitchen, but with substantial floor space and additional storage. This was a two-story house, so we had to make several structural changes to safely support the upper floor.

We found the best way to arrange the archway for best visibility was to place it at an angle at the end of the kitchen opposite the breakfast room door. That arrangement provided the most counter space, and easy access to the outside wall for venting. Since this home wasn't built on a concrete slab, we had to provide extra support for the brickwork.

Figure 7-3 B shows the archway containing the grill and cabinets and the center island. The center island is 60 inches long by 33 inches wide. It has a butcher block surface with an overhang that's deep enough so someone can sit while they work at the

B   Elevations

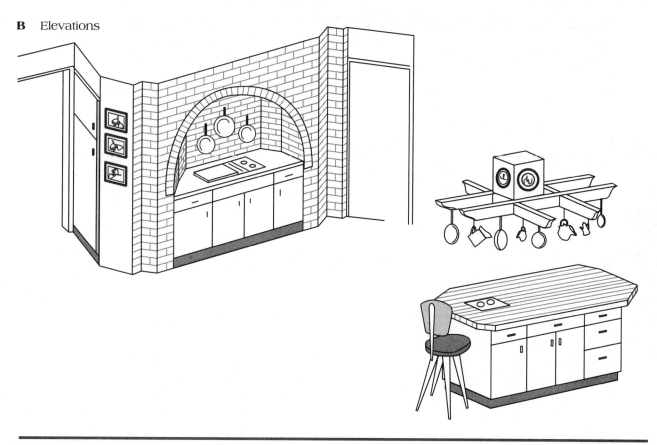

Figure 7-3 (cont.)
A layout designed to show off the brick-enclosed wall

island. There's also a food processing unit built into the countertop. We mounted a light fixture over the island and attached beams to the bottom of the fixture. Decorative hangers attached to these beams are used to display cookware and utensils.

We cantilevered the desk top to make cleaning under it much easier. The desk is set back a foot from the doorway so people aren't likely to bump into it.

Both the examples in this chapter show that kitchens don't have to be entirely conventional in shape or arrangement to be practical. Don't be afraid to use your imagination and creativity when designing or remodeling kitchens for your clients. Just stick to the Basic Rules. Homeowners spend a lot of time in the kitchen. They'll appreciate what you do to make that kitchen comfortable, attractive, and efficient.

Test Questions for Chapter 7

1. What is the biggest design flaw in the kitchen in Figure 7-1?

2. Name two other obvious errors in that kitchen.

3. What was gained by curving the sink wall cabinets?

4. How can you meet fire safety regulations when making the new closet behind the refrigerator open into the garage?

5. Give two reasons why the eating counter was made so deep.

6. The rolling cart at the end of the island provides flexibility. What feature in a kitchen would make it impractical?

7. What do you have to do if the existing floor can't support the weight of masonry around the wall oven?

8. In Figure 7-3 there's more brickwork surrounding the indoor grill. Why was the archway holding the grill set at an angle?

9. What did we do to the island to make it more useful?

10. What creative design opportunity does a light fixture over an island provide?

CHAPTER 8
Cabinets and Countertops

Once you've designed the layout for the perfect kitchen, it's time to furnish it. You'll begin with cabinets, then install the appliances and special features that make your kitchen design both functional and attractive.

The Evolution of Cabinetry

Every kitchen, no matter how small, needs space to store and protect cooking implements. In the home where I grew up, we had "cup-boards" in the kitchen. These were no more than small closets with shelves, usually built into the wall and made from solid wood. Cabinetmakers in the early 1900s used mostly solid pine, birch, or red oak, usually cut from green lumber that hadn't been properly seasoned. The result was cabinets that often warped and split. We know how to build better cabinets now.

Today, most lumber is seasoned on racks which allow air to circulate and dry the wood. Better quality wood is kiln-dried until the moisture content is about 8 percent – nearly bone-dry. But even the finest grades of dry wood tend to split and warp. And top grades of select species are always very expensive. Obviously, there was room for man to improve on what nature provided.

Most cabinets are now built of plywood, particleboard or cheaper lumber faced with veneer. These materials resist warping, are more plentiful, and are much less expensive than solid kiln-dried finish-grade lumber.

Figure 8-1 shows two types of laminated cabinet material. Plycore has a 5-ply core, faced with veneer. Lumber core has a solid wood core, and is usually faced on both sides with a single ply of veneer.

Manufacturers of top-grade cabinets use solid lumber core strips of seasoned basswood, joined electronically with waterproof glue, to form a solid core. For extra strength, a cross banding of poplar is added before the veneer. Oak is probably the most popular species for solid wood cabinets or veneer, followed by maple and birch. The last two look very much alike, but maple often has a cleaner, less fuzzy grain. Pine is suitable for a rustic country style. Occasionally more exotic woods are used.

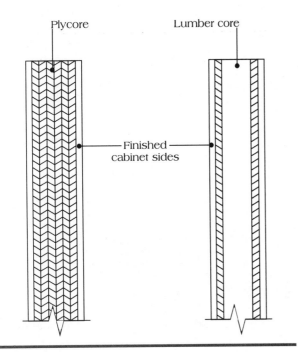

Figure 8-1
Laminated cabinet material

Measuring for Cabinets

Be extremely careful when you measure for cabinets. Accuracy is critical and mistakes are expensive. A miss of as little as a quarter of an inch can create big headaches for your cabinet installers. Measure first along the wall. Then measure again 24 inches out from the wall where the face of a standard base cabinet will rest. If the second measurement is less than the first, you can probably scribe the end stiles to make the cabinets fit. But you might have to order cabinets in sizes other than you originally planned.

Here's a good rule of thumb to follow when you measure for cabinets. Never assume that walls are flush and vertical, that walls on opposite ends of a room are parallel, that intersecting walls meet at a 90-degree angle, that the floor is level or that the ceiling is parallel to the floor. Usually, they aren't. Measure to be sure.

Figure 8-2 shows a simplified plan of a kitchen countertop I designed once for a small U-shaped kitchen. My subcontractor measured the kitchen and built the countertop. But apparently he didn't measure

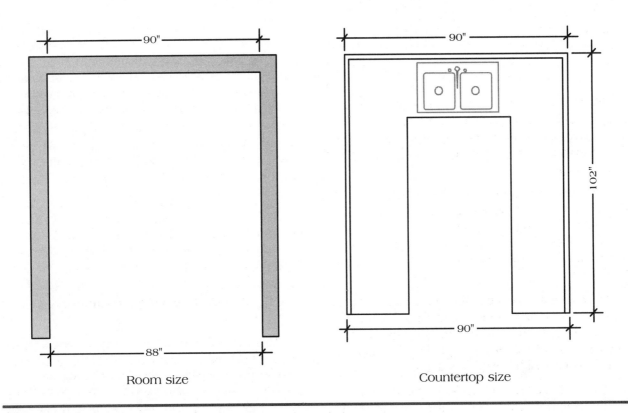

Figure 8-2
Measure each dimension carefully

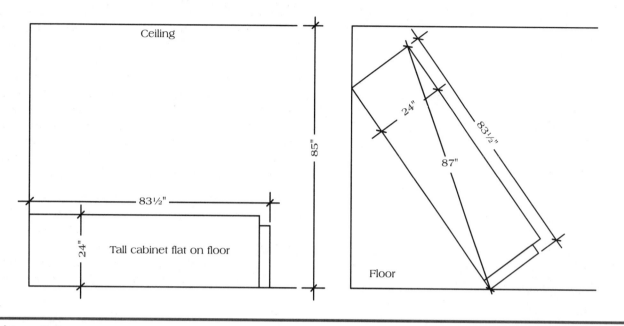

Figure 8-3
Plan ahead for installation

the distance between the walls at the open end of the U. He built the top in one piece, assuming the room was square. When the time came for installation, the installers couldn't warp the top enough to get it to fit at the open end of the U. The countertop had a full backsplash, so it wasn't possible to trim the top to fit. The entire countertop had to be rebuilt.

When you measure for cabinets, I recommend that you follow the procedure described in Chapter 1. Even better, get your countertop or cabinet subcontractor to accept responsibility for the accuracy of measurements.

Stock cabinets come in widths ranging from 9 to 48 inches. Order corner and end cabinets with extra material for scribing if you can. Standard sizes change in 3-inch increments. Base cabinets finish out at 36 inches high, and wall cabinets come in heights of 12 to 30 inches.

Choose base cabinets for sinks and cooktops according to the size of the appliance or fixture. Size other cabinets to best fit the available space with a minimum use of spacers, and particularly avoid the blank look created by spacers wider than 5 inches.

To check the level of the floor or ceiling, lay a 2 x 4 the length of the room on the floor or ceiling. Level the 2 x 4 and check for variations beneath it. On the floor, you can conceal small irregularities with a

cove strip, or run sheet flooring up onto the toe space. Another way is to scribe the toe kick to follow the irregularities.

Don't stop when you've taken all your lateral measurements. Take accurate vertical measurements as well. Your overall vertical measurement should be the minimum distance between the highest point on the floor and the lowest point on the ceiling. If a slab floor is severely uneven you can grind off the high spots or "float" the depressions with a concrete-like material available from your building materials dealer for that purpose.

Here's another common mistake. Look at Figure 8-3. I planned a floor-to-ceiling utility cabinet under a dropped ceiling. The cabinet could be brought into the home through a sliding glass door. The illustration of the left shows the cabinet resting flat on the floor. So far, so good. But we couldn't tip the cabinet upright once it was inside the room. See the illustration on the right in Figure 8-3.

The only solution was to remove the toe space base on the cabinet. That reduced the diagonal measurement of the cabinet from 87 to 84½ inches – short enough to clear the ceiling. Once the cabinet was upright, we could raise the cabinet into position, brace it from below, secure it to the wall, and reattach the toeboard.

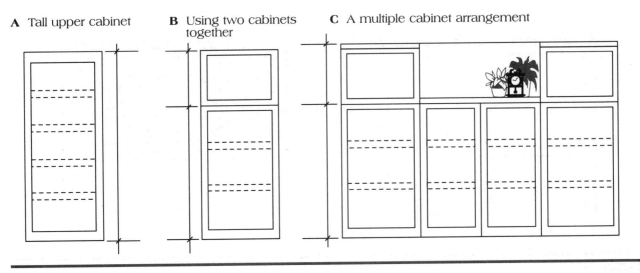

A Tall upper cabinet   **B** Using two cabinets together   **C** A multiple cabinet arrangement

Figure 8-4
Use tall uppers when there's no soffit

Cabinets to the Ceiling, or Not?

In kitchens without a dropped ceiling or soffit, you have several options for the height of the upper cabinets.

◆ Extend them all the way to a standard 8-foot ceiling

◆ Extend them as high as is practical when the ceiling is higher than 8 feet

◆ Use a standard 24- or 30-inch upper, and place another cabinet above it.

Figure 8-4 A shows a standard tall upper cabinet, which can be any height, provided the doors aren't so long that warping might be a problem. I don't recommend using cabinets with doors taller than 5 feet. Figures 8-4 B and 8-4 C illustrate two ways to use cabinets one above the other.

High cabinets are hard to get at, so they're useful only for storing seldom-used things. But where storage space is scarce, the inconvenience is tolerable.

There's a significant difference in cost between a single cabinet 8 feet high and two cabinets totaling 8 feet high. A single cabinet is much cheaper. However, some clients are willing to spend the extra money, especially in an arrangement like the one in Figure 8-4 C.

I avoid using cabinets that extend to the ceiling if there's an obstruction in the center. For instance, a surface-mounted light fixture, decorative or supporting beam, or HVAC vent might interfere with a cabinet door if it's too close. If you must place cabinets near an obstruction, use sliding doors as in Figure 8-5. Recessed finger pulls allow the doors to pass without colliding.

Consider installing stained glass panels in high cabinets. Then put a fluorescent light at the top back of the cabinet. That illuminates the glass panel like sunlight coming through a church window.

Cabinet Door Designs

Cabinet door designs have improved a lot since I was a boy. I can remember cabinets with surface-mounted batten doors. The doors were simply several vertical boards held together by crosswise battens. Today nearly every manufacturer offers dozens of styles. Figure 8-6 shows several of them.

Not all kitchen cabinet doors are made of wood. Some are made of furniture grade steel with full double pan construction. Mastic-coated wood battens, running the length of the door, are bonded between steel panels. The entire assembly is cured under pressure at high temperature, then welded to form a rigid, smooth, flush surface inside and out. Then the manufacturer applies a synthetic enamel, specially prepared for kitchen use. The result is a smooth finish in a variety of colors. St. Charles Kitchens is one manufacturer these cabinets.

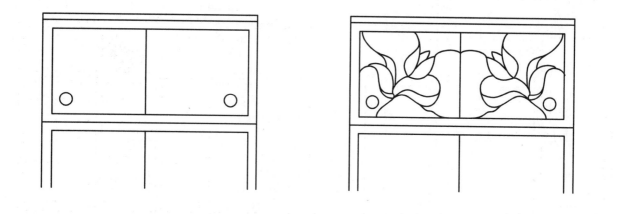

Figure 8-5

Sliding cabinet doors work when there's no room for hinged doors

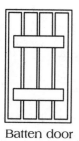 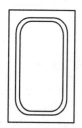 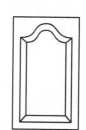

Batten door   Raised panel   Beaded door   French provincial

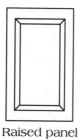  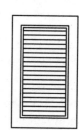 

Routed door   Random plank   Gothic or   Hawaiian shutter
                                            cathedral

 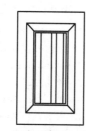 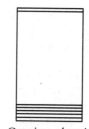

Valencia moorish   Raised panel   Grecian classic   Oval gothic
                     random cut

Figure 8-6

Cabinet doors come in a variety of styles

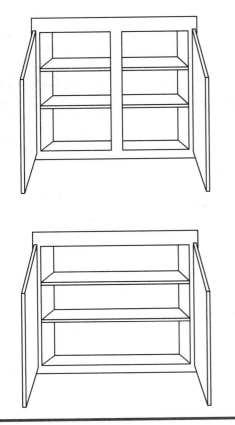

Figure 8-7
Avoid stiles if you can

Other manufacturers build cabinet and door panels surfaced with tempered Masonite on both sides and with a seasoned wood core. They come in either a high gloss or matte finish.

Avoid Stiles If You Can

Figure 8-7 shows the advantage of eliminating the center stile in cabinets. If the shelf is full, something is sure to be behind the stile. Then you have to move something from either side of the stile to get at what's behind it.

When cabinet shelves were made of solid lumber, the stile was needed in wide cabinets to keep the shelves from sagging. Today's metal, fiberboard, plywood or flakeboard shelves don't warp or bend under normal loads, even when they're as wide as 42 inches.

There's one disadvantage to double door cabinets without a stile if you use matching natural-finished doors. If one door is damaged (or defective), you'll have to replace both doors to retain the continuity in the grain pattern.

If you object to the gap between the doors, you can attach a cleat to make a "false stile" at the back of one of the doors. Glue a ¼-inch-thick strip of wood that matches the cabinet door finish and height to the inside of one door. The strip only needs to be a couple of inches wide. Now the closed doors appear to have a stile behind them. The only disadvantage is that if you open the cleated door first, the other door pops open too.

Cabinet Shelving and Drawers

Less expensive cabinets usually have fixed shelves. Better quality cabinets have adjustable shelves. Shelves often rest on plastic seats that plug into holes drilled in the cabinet sides. They can be adjusted at intervals of 2 inches. Shelves that rest on a support inserted into a perforated metal strip can be adjusted with half-inch precision. The metal strips are recessed in more expensive cabinets, surface mounted in others.

Drawer quality also varies by cost. In less expensive drawers, the bottoms are Masonite sheets which slide into a groove. Drawer frames are often pine or basswood, simply stapled together. Higher-quality drawers are usually made with dovetailed or dadoed joints and bottoms of ⅜- to ½-inch birch. Figure 8-8 shows both types of drawer construction.

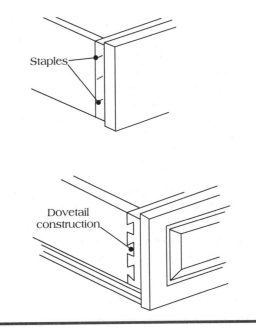

Figure 8-8
Better quality doors are dovetailed, not stapled

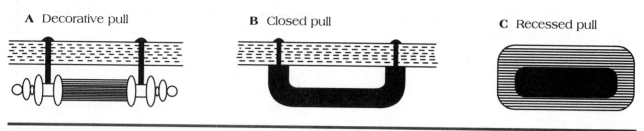

A Decorative pull   **B** Closed pull   **C** Recessed pull

Figure 8-9
Cabinet and drawer hardware comes in many styles and finishes

In cheaper cabinets, the drawers slide on a center guide. More expensive cabinets have side-mounted, wrap-around captive drawer slides that are self-closing with a positive stop. Heavy-duty nylon rollers ensure smooth performance for many years. Other good quality cabinets are made of heavy gauge die-formed interlocking slides with nylon rollers inclined at the back so they're self-closing.

Hardware

There's an enormous variety of cabinet hardware available. You'll find hundreds of designs and finishes for every purpose and every decorative style. Every design showroom, builder's supply, and hardware store carries cabinet hardware in many types and colors.

When you choose cabinet hardware, my advice is to avoid pulls with protruding ends, as in Figure 8-9 A. Of course, some decorating schemes seem to demand this type of decorative hardware. But those exposed ends seem to have an uncanny attraction for sleeves, pockets, dishtowels and apron strings. I prefer closed handles like in Figure 8-9 B. Even better, use recessed pulls, as in Figure 8-9 C. Today, many cabinets have pulls built in as part of the cabinet design and require no pull hardware at all.

Cabinet hardware comes in brass, copper, and bronze finishes, chrome, stainless steel, aluminum, wood, porcelain, ceramic and even precious metals. You can get pulls and handles in a variety of colors, or stained to match the cabinet's finish.

Cabinet Door Catches

Spring catches (as in Figure 8-10 A) are considered obsolete today. They're noisy and the springs tend to bend or break. Magnetic catches (as in Figure

A Spring latch

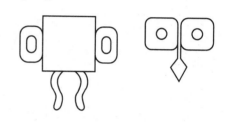

B Magnetic latch

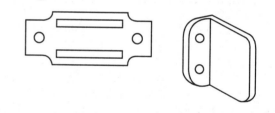

Figure 8-10
Spring and magnetic cabinet door latches

8-10 B) are much more practical. Touch latches are also available, but I like to avoid them in kitchens because of the finger marks they attract. You can buy spring hinges that eliminate the need for magnets or other mechanical fasteners.

For situations where protection of small children is an issue, Rev-A-Shelf® produces a convenient security lock which features a magnetic "key" for cabinets. For information, call 1-800-626-1126.

Cabinet Finishes

Modern finishes are both attractive and require very little maintenance. Years ago, there were only two choices: an oil finish to bring out the grain of the wood, or a lacquer finish. They're still available, of course. But today's versions of these finishes are far more durable and maintenance-free.

Top quality natural finish cabinets are sanded, stained and hand-wiped to bring out the natural beauty of the wood. After a sealer coat is applied, it's lightly sanded and cleaned. Then an oven-cured top coat is applied to give the same type of finish as on fine furniture. The final finish is a catalytic conversion varnish, which many feel is the ultimate in finish coatings.

For an enameled finish on wood cabinets, the base is given two catalyzed pigmented sealer coats and a pigmented enamel top coat.

Laminated plastic cabinets are finished as they're formed. Resin finishes such as Melamine provide superior wearing qualities ideal for a kitchen.

Adding to Existing Cabinets

Some of your clients may want to add new cabinets without replacing existing ones. If the new cabinets will butt against cabinets already there, you'll have to match the finish. That's seldom easy, whether the existing cabinets are stained, laminate or have an enamel finish. Even if you use the same color stain, paint or laminate, there will be differences because the older cabinets almost certainly have faded, discolored or show wear.

One option is to strip the existing cabinets and refinish them to match the new ones. That's an expensive, messy, and time-consuming job. It might be better to re-face the existing cabinets. In that case, refinish just the cabinet frames and replace the cabinet drawer and door fronts with the same design as the new cabinets.

If the new cabinets will stand alone in another part of the room, you can probably get away with a subtle variation in color, and perhaps even a sight difference in the style of cabinet face.

Pantry Cabinets

Whenever possible, find room in the kitchen for a pantry cabinet. It's always more convenient to have storage for staple items close at hand, rather than in another room, or worse yet, the garage. Sometimes there's no choice but to have a pantry elsewhere because of limited space, but put it inside the kitchen if you can.

Too often, kitchen pantries are enclosed in a closet. That's an unnecessary waste of space – the almost 10 inches of enclosing wall space could be better used for larger cabinets. A closet-type pantry might be appropriate when it's outside the kitchen, but avoid it otherwise.

It's natural to assume that the larger the cabinet, the more it will hold. But that isn't always the case. A large pantry with stationary shelves placed too far apart won't hold nearly as much as a smaller one with adjustable shelves in varying widths. The extra flexibility yields much more real storage space. When you design a pantry, make it as large as you can. But be sure most users can easily see and reach what's stored there.

The 18-inch Pantry

A pantry that's only 18 inches wide can still be useful. It's all in the way it's arranged. Install as many roll-out shelves as you can. But don't put shelves above eye level. Use the space above eye level for a cabinet with adjustable movable dividers to store large, flat items on edge.

Figure 8-11 shows the location and layout of a pantry like this. Notice the counter space immediately to the left of the pantry. That's a convenient landing place for unloading grocery bags or removing items stored in the pantry.

Roll-out shelves come with a lip at the back and sides to keep things from sliding off. Many manufacturers today offer storage systems featuring coated wire baskets and drawers which provide almost limitless installation options. If you install stationary shelves, space them not less than 9 inches apart.

The 24-inch Special Pantry

Figure 8-12 shows a pantry design suitable for a 24- or 30-inch-wide space. Don't go any wider than that – shelves will be too heavy to handle. The center bar is designed to pull out all shelves at once. You can see everything at one time, without pulling out the shelves one by one. Heavy-duty tracks installed in the top and bottom of the cabinet support this unit.

I don't recommend this pantry for a space less than 24 inches wide. The shelf space on either side of the center bar would be too small to be of much use.

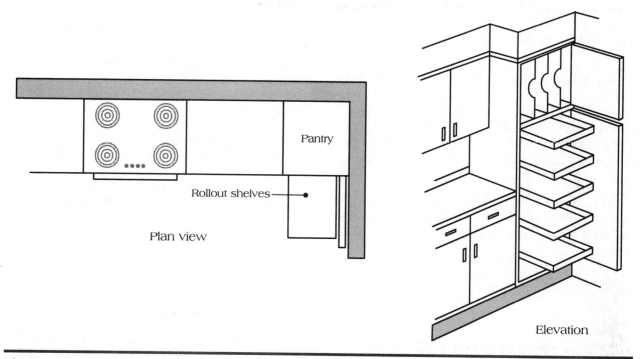

Figure 8-11
Convenient pantry layout with nearby countertop

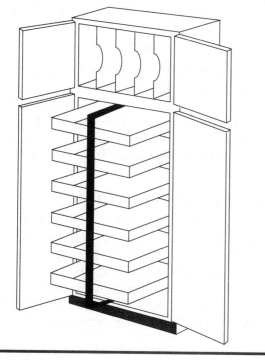

Figure 8-12
All these pantry shelves slide out at once

The 36-inch Pantry

Figure 8-13 shows a pantry cabinet that combines maximum storage space with excellent visibility and access. The inner shelves swing out for easy access. So this cabinet, like a refrigerator with shelves in the door, can't be restricted by the wall beside it. The doors must open a full 180 degrees.

The 15-inch Pullout Full-Height Pantry

Even a space as small as 15 inches wide can hold a spacious pantry. Figure 8-14 shows an example. This pantry is divided vertically, off-center, so there are two sets of shelves back-to-back. On one side, the shelves are deep enough to hold cereal boxes. The narrow shelves on the opposite side are suitable for canned goods or small packages. This pantry glides out on heavy duty rollers installed in the top and bottom of the cabinet.

Be sure the supporting assembly is adequate to carry the weight when this cabinet is loaded with groceries. If the track pulls out, the unit may jam in the cabinet. Then it's useless.

Figure 8-13
A roomy pantry where everything is at the front of the shelf

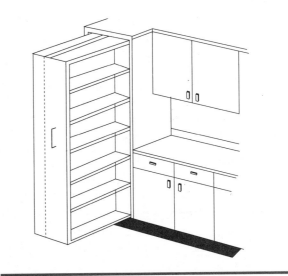

Figure 8-14
This pantry is suspended on a track system . . .

Figure 8-15 shows a similar pantry cabinet, but this one rides on casters with guides to keep it moving in a straight line. It works best on a perfectly flat surface such as vinyl or hardwood. It's not suitable for installation on carpeting, or on an uneven floor like ceramic tile or pavers.

St Charles® cabinets offer many of these features, and others, as modular units.

The Under-Counter Pantry

If there's not enough room for a tall pantry, consider installing a pantry cabinet under the counter. It can be as narrow as 12 inches if you put it at the end of a counter, island, or peninsula so the door is on the 24-inch side. If a pantry this small opens from the 12-inch side, there's little usable space remaining after the track assemblies and shelf enclosure sides are installed. Figure 8-16 shows plan and elevation views for an under-counter pantry.

The Off-Kitchen Pantry

Pantry closets can be quite small and still be useful. As little as 9 square feet may be plenty. Shelving should be attached to the wall opposite the door as in Figure 8-17 A. If there's enough space, shallow shelves may wrap around, though this arrangement leaves corners which aren't easily accessible. Figure 8-17 B shows this layout. Walk-in pantry shelves can be anywhere from 12 to 20 inches deep. Leave enough space between lowest and highest shelves to

store a tall cereal box. Middle shelves can be closer together. Movable shelves are best.

Pantry closets seldom have nearby counter space. If that's the case, build a pull-out shelf into the pantry itself. There's more information about this in Chapter 1. Mount the retractable shelf under a stationary shelf about 36 inches above the floor. That makes it easy to

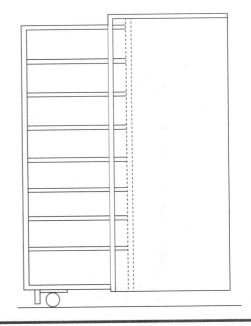

Figure 8-15
. . . while this one glides out on casters

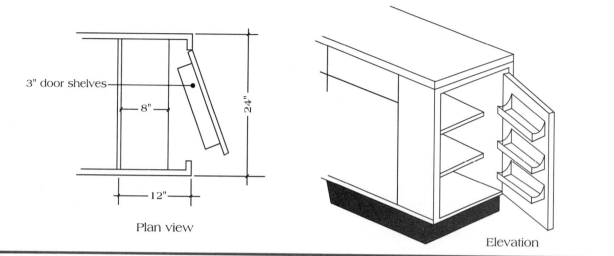

Plan view

3" door shelves

8"

24"

12"

Elevation

Figure 8-16
A compact under-counter pantry

pull out the shelf when you need a place to set a gro-cery bag or assemble items for removal to the kitchen. Hang a tray somewhere in the pantry, or on the door, to carry things back and forth.

Lazy Susan Cabinets

Lazy Susan cabinets are standard items with many cabinet manufacturers, and come in many styles. They consist of two round shelves, supported by a spindle in the center, which rotate within the cab-inet. The shelves usually have a pie-shaped wedge cut out of them.

Lazy Susan base cabinets are designed to fit in corners and usually measure 36 inches wide along each wall. The biggest difference between lazy Susan designs is the way you open them. Some have a dou-ble hinged door as in Figure 8-18 A. In others, the door is attached to the shelves and rotates with them as shown in Figure 8-18 B. In Figure 8-18 C, the cab-inet has a diagonal corner face with a door which can be hinged on either side. The shelves in this cabinet don't have the wedge cut out.

If you use the base style as in Figure 8-18 C, use a diagonal corner wall cabinet as well. Otherwise, it will be too hard to reach the face of the upper cabinet. Figure 8-19 A shows the correct corner wall cabinet. Figure 8-19 B shows what happens if you install a regular corner cabinet.

A One shelf

Shelf

B Wraparound shelves

Dead corner

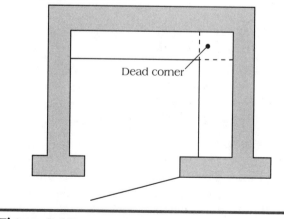

Figure 8-17
Enclosed pantry closets

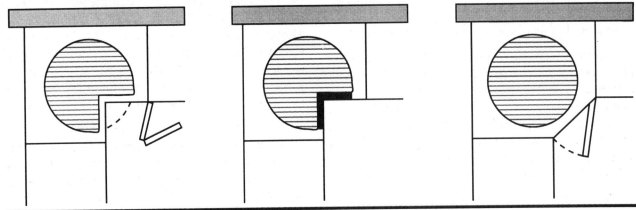

A Double hinged door   **B** Door rotates with lazy Susan   **C** Diagonal cabinet with door

Figure 8-18
Lazy Susan variations

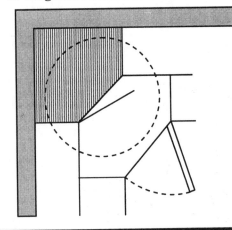

A Diagonal corner wall cabinet

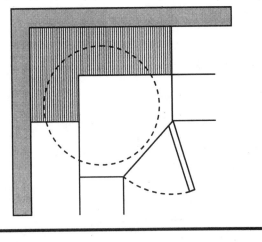

B Wall cabinets out of reach

Figure 8-19
Use a corner upper cabinet to bring shelves within reach

Installing Cabinets

Always try to schedule two carpenters to install cabinets. Cabinets and countertops are usually too awkward to handle alone. A crew of two reduces the risk of damage to cabinets during installation.

Before you begin, mark on the wall the height of the base cabinets, the location for the bottom of the upper cabinets, and the soffit location (if a soffit is to be installed later). Start by locating studs that will support the cabinets. If you're experienced – and the wallboard isn't too thick – you can probably find studs by rapping on the wall with your knuckles. Then drive

the tip of a long 10d nail into the wall until you hit the stud. Do this at a level where the cabinets will cover the holes. (Fill any "misses" with putty.) Once you locate one stud, you'll usually find others spaced each 16 inches along the entire wall. Rarely, they're 24 inches apart.

If you're hanging cabinets on masonry or concrete walls, use masonry anchors to secure the cabinet mounting screws.

Always install the upper cabinets first. Obviously, it's easier to hang wall cabinets without base cabinets in the way. There are two ways to support the cabinets before you fasten them to the wall. First, you can nail a wood strip to the wall just below the wall cabinet. While a helper holds the cabinet in place while it's resting on this strip, screw the cabinet to the wall.

A better way is to build a platform to support the uppers. Use 2 x 4s for the legs to support a 2 x 8 plank platform. Make this support the height of the bottom of the upper cabinets. Level the support platform with shims under the legs until it's exactly the right height. This method is especially helpful if you're installing a series of upper cabinets and attaching them together as one. Figure 8-20 illustrates this support in use.

When the walls aren't straight, you'll have to shim the cabinets to make them flush, level and plumb. Once they're aligned, clamp them firmly together. Drill through the stiles on adjacent cabinets, then countersink #6 screws, 2½ or 3 inches long, from one cabinet into the next one. The screws should penetrate the receiving stile, but not go all the way through it.

In most upper cabinets, the top and bottom shelves are recessed slightly from the wall, leaving a small lip at the back. Drill through this lip and drive #6 screws, again 2½ or 3 inches long, into the wall stud. Countersink the screws, or use a round head screw and washer. Don't completely tighten the screws until you've checked for plumb. Shim the cabinet if necessary, and then tighten down the screws.

You may also have to use shims, or trim the stiles, where cabinets go around a corner. Corners are rarely exactly 90 degrees. Some adjustment will almost always be necessary to make the cabinets line up properly.

Install base cabinets about the same way as you install wall cabinets. Connect the bases together, and make sure they're level both lengthwise and front to back. If the cabinets are longer than the available space, you'll have to trim off some of the end stiles. If they're slightly shorter, fill the gap with molding finished to match the cabinets.

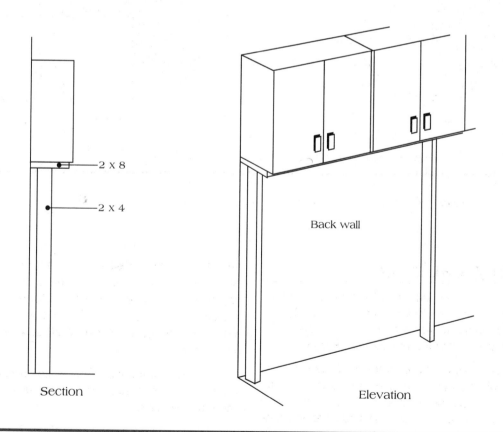

2 x 8

2 x 4

Section

Back wall

Elevation

Figure 8-20
Build a support to hold the uppers while you install them

Countertops

Modern work surfaces are a big improvement over the linoleum used when I first started in the construction business. Today's materials are both durable and beautiful.

Countertop Materials

In this section we'll cover the most popular countertop materials.

Formica™   This plastic laminate material is widely used for countertops, cabinets and furniture. In fact, it's used nearly anywhere a non-porous, durable, smooth surface is needed. It comes in an almost unlimited range of colors and patterns, and in textures from high gloss to embossed. It has two disadvantages. First, under high heat, it will scorch, or even blister and crack. And, it can chip if you drop something sharp and heavy on it.

Small chips can be repaired with commercial compounds made for that purpose. Your building material dealer will have several recommendations. Larger damaged areas have to be replaced. You can cut out the damaged area and insert a section of tile, stainless steel, marble or wood. If that's not possible, you'll have to replace the entire countertop.

Avoid using high-gloss patterns for countertops. They show every finger mark and water spot, and light reflecting off them can be annoying. Use a matte finish instead.

Corners and joints in older Formica countertops were usually protected by a metal molding. Now, edges and joints are rolled for a smooth, one-piece finish.

Most builders today install counters with a 4-inch backsplash to save money. I recommend a full backsplash that extends all the way to the underside of the upper cabinets. That saves a lot of cleaning, painting or paper hanging labor around countertop work spaces. Behind a cooktop, extend the backsplash all the way up to the range hood.

A 4-inch backsplash is usually made with extra material at the top so you can scribe it to fit the contour of the wall. Figure 8-21 is a cross section of a short countertop showing the overcut on the backsplash. A full backsplash doesn't have any extra material for scribing, and the top is unfinished. If there's a gap between the backsplash and the wall when the top is mounted, cut a strip of countertop material wide enough to fill the gap.

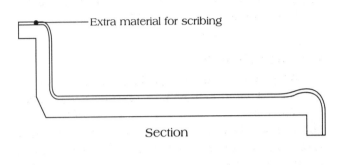

Figure 8-21
Laminated countertops have a trim allowance

Corian   Made by DuPont, this is acrylic with aluminum fillers. You can sand out scratches if they aren't too deep.

Avonite   This is a pure polyester material made in more than 20 colors by the Avonite Company. It has a stone-like finish and can be polished to a high gloss.

Fountainhead   This material, made by Nevamar, has some of the characteristics of both Avonite and Corian. It's made of acrylic polyester and aluminum fillers and comes in nine colors. Its stone finishes can be polished to a high gloss.

Glazed Ceramic Tile   Tile is a great favorite with decorators because it comes in so many colors and designs. It's colorful, heat resistant, and durable. It's harder to maintain than a laminated plastic surface because the grout spaces tend to collect dirt. But many people are willing to tolerate the inconvenience in exchange for the added durability and rich appearance. Tile does chip, however. So when you install tile tops, leave a few extra tiles and edge pieces with the owner. They'll appreciate your thoughtfulness.

Glazed ceramic tile makes a good countertop. But I never recommend unglazed tile with more porous surfaces, such as Talavera and unglazed Saltillo. They're too bumpy and uneven to make even a temporary countertop work surface.

Butcher Block   You can get butcher block inserts in hard birch, oak, and other hardwoods. Most are 2 to 4 inches thick, though I've seen block up to 8 inches thick.

Simulated Granite   Simulated granite countertops called Polymer-Granite Stone are also available.

These tops tend to be expensive, but may be a good choice where the owner wants a unique kitchen. Simulated granite is said to be the most scratch, stain and heat resistant countertop made.

Counter Savers

When you install plastic laminate countertops, it's a good idea to provide a counter saver, either built-in or portable, to protect the countertop from burns. Portable counter savers are tempered glass sheets that are extremely durable, heat- and scratch-resistant and come in several sizes. Some brands come in colors.

Besides providing a place to set hot pots and pans, counter savers make good cutting boards and are a handy place to roll dough. Put a counter saver next to the cooking surface, between the cooktop and a wall oven, or next to the microwave.

Install counter savers flush with the countertop surrounded by a rim of the type often used to surround a sink.

Installing Countertops

Sometimes it's impossible to bring a countertop into the kitchen in one piece. In that case, take the top apart at the corners. Then reassemble it using draw bolts installed for that purpose at the factory.

Sometimes you can get a big countertop in place by passing it through a window opening. I've done that successfully even when the kitchen was on the second floor. But sometimes the most sensible and cost-effective solution is to simply build the countertop in place.

If you use a prefabricated plastic-laminate countertop, attach it to the cabinets with screws from below. Just be sure the screws aren't so long that they contact (or worse yet, penetrate) the covering material.

Most base cabinets have corner braces of wood or particleboard. Drive screws through those and into the countertop base. Don't glue the countertop to the base cabinets. That makes it nearly impossible to remove the base cabinet without doing major damage.

Test Questions for Chapter 8

1. How is most lumber seasoned? How is better-quality lumber seasoned?

2. Name two types of laminated cabinet material used today.

3. Why is it especially important to be very careful when measuring for cabinets?

4. What is a good rule to keep in mind when measuring for cabinets and countertops?

5. Why is it necessary to remove the toe space base before tilting a floor-to-ceiling cabinet into place?

6. What's the disadvantage of having a stile separate two doors of a cabinet?

7. What's the major difference between less expensive and more expensive drawers?

8. When installing an under-counter pantry that's only 12 inches deep, why should it open from the widest side?

9. When the base corner cabinet is angled, why should the upper cabinet above it also be angled?

10. Which should you install first, the upper or the lower cabinets?

CHAPTER 9
Sinks and Plumbing

The kitchen is the center of activity in many households. It's the most frequent meeting place for most families. And the sink is the focal point of the kitchen. People need access to water for food preparation and cleanup, for housekeeping chores, for drinking and beverage mixing, for washing their hands, and for doing hand laundry. People use the kitchen sink to water house plants, shampoo their hair, and sometimes to bathe a baby or the family pet. The variety of uses for the kitchen sink is the main reason for Basic Rule #1 – there must be plenty of counter space on both sides of the kitchen sink.

Types of Sinks

Sinks come in a wide range of sizes, colors, shapes, materials and layouts. Some people prefer a single, large sink, while others favor a sink with two or more smaller compartments. Many models come with a choice of two, three or four fixture openings in case you want to install a drinking-water spout or soap/lotion dispenser in addition to the dishwasher air gap. If you later need to plug one of these openings, you can do so with a special cap available from plumbing supply houses.

The Single-Bowl Sink

Where counter space is limited, a single 24 x 21-inch sink like the one shown in Figure 9-1 is a good choice. The basin is big enough to hold oven racks or a roasting pan, and there's only one drain to install and maintain. The garbage disposer is in the center of the sink or can be mounted toward the rear. The sink cabinet needs to be only 27 inches wide, so there's room for larger adjacent cabinets.

Figure 9-2 shows a single-compartment sink with a disposal well in one corner. This is handy for preparing and rinsing fruits and vegetables. One advantage here is that there's not so much danger of dropping silverware or other small objects down the garbage disposer when you're washing dishes. The disadvantage is that the main basin is smaller – maybe too small for the largest utensils.

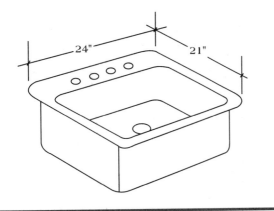

Figure 9-1
A single-bowl sink

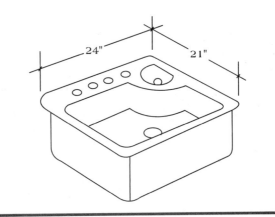

Figure 9-2
This sink features a disposal well

Single sinks also come in a 30-inch width that fits into a 32-inch base cabinet. For normal dishwashing and rinsing, the homeowner can create a divided sink by setting a plastic dishpan in one side of the sink.

The Two-Bowl Sink

Figure 9-3 shows a standard two-bowl sink with basins the same size. The disposer unit can be mounted in either side. This sink setup requires a 36-inch base cabinet, so it's not the best choice for a very limited space. The two-bowl sink is also available in a 42-inch width.

Figure 9-4 shows a better arrangement. Here the larger basin will hold a large pan or oven rack, and the smaller one is handy for rinsing food or dishes.

The Three-Bowl Sink

Cooks who do a lot of entertaining, or feed a large family, often prefer the three-sink layout in Figure 9-5. This provides space for:

1) Soaking or rinsing dishes before placing them in the dishwasher

2) Preparing fresh fruits and vegetables

3) A "to-clean" sink for dirty cooking utensils

The only drawback is that neither of the large basins is big enough to hold large pans, mixing bowls or oven racks. But it's handier than the standard two-bowl sink because a large pan or oven rack can "straddle" the center section, dripping into the sink, not onto the floor or countertop. This arrangement requires a 45- to 48-inch base cabinet.

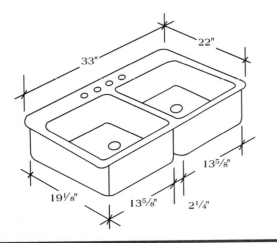

Figure 9-3
A standard twin-bowl sink

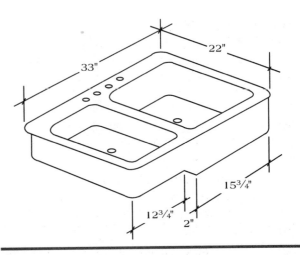

Figure 9-4
Different-sized sinks in the same space as
twin-bowl sink

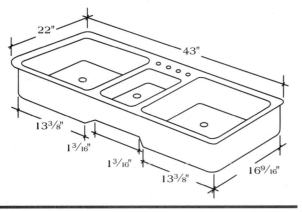

Figure 9-5
Three bowls add convenience

Corner Sinks

Figure 9-6 shows a corner sink with the basins at right angles. This layout is best where there are corner windows because the windows and window sills are within easy reach.

You can also install a standard 33-inch double sink diagonally in a corner. If you do, use a minimum 5-inch filler between the sink front and the dishwasher. Otherwise there won't be room to stand at the sink with the dishwasher door open. Also set the sink as close to the wall as possible, or it's too hard to reach the back of the corner. Figure 9-7 shows the correct layout.

Don't install a sink wider than 33 inches diagonally in a corner. That would waste too much cabinet space on each side of the corner, and the sink would protrude too far into the room.

Secondary Sinks

Many modern kitchens have an auxiliary sink that serves a plant care center or wet bar, or makes an island or peninsula more convenient. These vary in size from full-sized to tiny sinks only 6 by 10 inches. They may be rectangular, round, triangular, oval or half-circles. Like a kitchen's primary sink, they can be molded with the countertop, or finished with enamel, metal, or even tile.

When you install a sink on an island or peninsula, be especially careful to follow Basic Rule #1. Place the sink so there's counter space on both sides. Never put the sink on the end of the counter.

Plumbing for an island sink or a newly-installed peninsula is a little different from plumbing on a main

A Basins at right angles

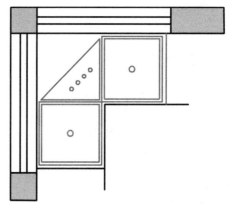

B Sink placed diagonally

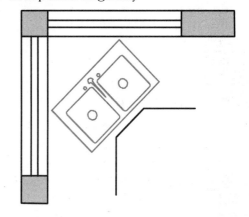

Figure 9-6
Two ways to arrange sinks in a corner

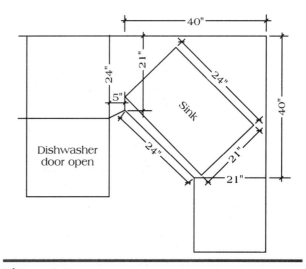

Figure 9-7
Recess a diagonal sink

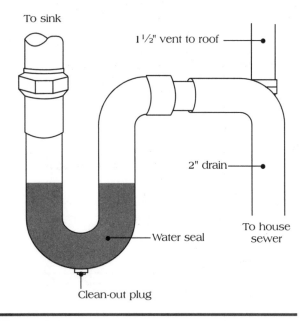

To sink

1 1/2" vent to roof

2" drain

Water seal

To house sewer

Clean-out plug

Figure 9-8
The P-trap provides a water seal barrier to air and sewer gases

sink. Since it's not against a wall, all the supply, vent and drain lines have to be run below floor level. If there's a crawl space, that's no problem. But if the room is built on a slab, you have to cut a channel in the concrete to house the plumbing lines.

Sink Materials

There are three major categories of kitchen sinks: enameled cast iron or pressed metal, stainless steel, and integral molded sinks of Corian or marble formed as part of the countertop. We'll take a look at the advantages and disadvantages of each.

Enameled Sinks

Enameled cast iron is still the most popular material for sinks today. You can also get sinks made of enameled pressed metal. These are less expensive than their cast iron counterparts because they're not as sturdy and the enamel coating isn't as thick.

Lighter-weight pressed metal sinks are more flexible than cast iron, so they're more prone to chipping. You can tell the difference between these and cast-iron sinks by rapping on the bowl bottom with your

knuckles. The pressed metal sink makes a sound like a bell. A cast iron sink makes a dull thump.

A chipped enamel-clad sink can be repaired with epoxy filler available at larger plumbing supply houses. But you're unlikely to get a perfect color match.

Enameled sinks come in a wide range of colors. Some have a rolled, raised edge that rests above the counter. Many homeowners don't like raised edges because it's hard to sweep spills into the sink. I recommend sinks you can install below countertop level.

Stainless Steel

Stainless steel sinks come in 18 and 22 gauge material. The 18 gauge is the heavier, more durable of the two. The higher nickel content makes it more wear resistant. While stainless steel sinks are cheaper than enamel and won't chip like enamel, they have disadvantages.

◆ They show water spots, requiring constant wiping dry to look good.

◆ It's possible to scratch the surface, but nearly impossible to polish out the scratches.

◆ Water splashing into a lightweight sink at high pressure makes a pounding sound.

◆ Some household cleaners and solvents can discolor them.

Stainless steel sinks usually aren't as deep as enamel sinks – about 2 inches shallower. You can get deep ones but they may cost more. If you plan a steel sink, install a faucet with a nozzle that's high enough so you can get a large pitcher, pot or bucket under it.

Stainless steel sinks come in brushed or polished finishes. Their biggest advantage is, as the name implies, that food residue won't penetrate and stain the finish.

Integral Molded Sinks

If you install a Corian or marble countertop, an integral sink will probably be an available option. If offered, and if your client can afford it, I recommend using a molded sink. If there's ever serious damage to a molded Corian sink, the damaged area can be cut out and replaced. It's also possible to repair simulated marble, or natural marble if a chip isn't too deep.

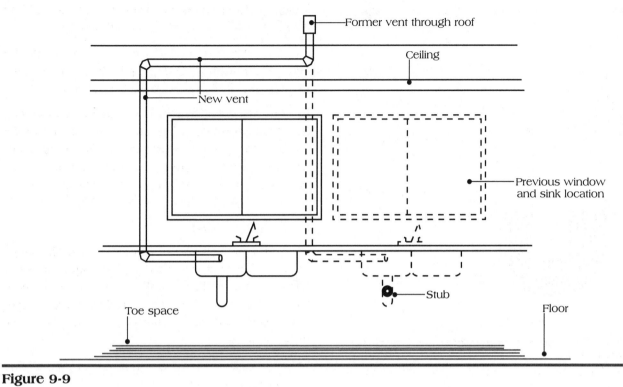

Figure 9-9
Route the vent pipe around the new window

Plumbing for Sinks

Every sink must have a trap between the sink and the drain. The trap provides a water seal to keep sewer gas out of the house. Figure 9-8 shows a typical P-trap. Where the drain enters the waste line, the plumbing code requires a vent to the roof of the building. This vent relieves back pressure and helps preserve the water seal. In some climates and under some codes, this vent pipe may have to be 3 inches in diameter so it doesn't get clogged with snow or ice.

Venting the kitchen sink can be a problem when you want the sink in front of a window. And when you remodel a kitchen and move the sink (and window), you'll have to move the vent.

I was faced with this problem, and managed to avoid installing an entirely new vent to the roof. Figure 9-9 shows how I rerouted the vent without disturbing the exit pipe, the shield apron, and the original roofing. The dotted lines show the original location of the window and sink, and the vent pipe. We had to secure the vent at the roof, since the supporting stem was removed in the process.

Instant Hot Water Units

It's very convenient to have boiling hot water instantly available at the sink, and several manufacturers offer instant hot water units. The one I recommend is the In-Sink-Erator brand, which has a tank attached to the cold water line. It refills itself as water is used, so there's a constant supply of 190-degree water available at the turn of a knob. The half gallon tank, which plugs into a normal 120 volt outlet, can supply up to 60 cups of instant hot water. While boiling water in the microwave is quick and inexpensive, the homeowner who frequently uses a cup or two of boiling water may want the convenience of instant availability.

As a kitchen designer, be sure to keep abreast of the latest developments in plumbing appliances and fixtures. New products come on the market every day to enhance the appearance and convenience of the modern kitchen. Also be aware of water conservation requirements. In some places, flow restrictors are required by code, and you may not be able to install certain types of water softeners or purification systems. Keep up with plumbing innovations and local restrictions, or your competitors might leave you high and dry.

Test Questions for Chapter 9

1. What is the best kind of sink to use when counter space is limited?

2. What variation makes the standard two-bowl sink even more practical?

3. While a three-bowl sink is extra useful for homes with large families, there are a couple of disadvantages. What are they?

4. What should you add when installing a corner sink with a dishwasher next to it?

5. Where might you install secondary sinks?

6. What are the disadvantages of stainless steel sinks?

7. Why are sinks installed below countertop level and integral molded sinks preferable to sinks with a raised edge?

8. When you install a sink in an island or peninsula on a slab floor, where do you run the plumbing lines?

9. How would you prevent sewer gas from entering the house?

10. How might local water conservation requirements affect what you may design into a kitchen?

CHAPTER 10
Major Appliances and Exhaust Systems

Today's ranges, cooktops and ovens are a far cry from those of only a few years ago, and revolutionary when compared to the wood- and coal-burning stoves our grandparents relied on. While the function remains the same – to heat foods to the right temperature to cook them properly – the method has changed drastically. Modern technology, materials and manufacturing methods provide today's cooks with flexibility and convenience that was unheard-of even a few years ago.

Cooking Appliances

Cooking appliances now come in a nearly endless variety of designs, sizes, colors, finishes, and layouts. The trick is to choose, from all those available, the features which best suit your client's needs.

Freestanding Ranges

Ranges which combine oven, broiler, cooktop, and sometimes a storage drawer, warming compartment and microwave in one freestanding unit are still popular today. Fueled by gas or electricity, they're compact, well insulated, and offer all the features and accessories found in their modular counterparts.

Freestanding ranges come in sizes ranging from 18 inches wide up to 4 feet or more. The smallest are a good choice for apartments or "kitchenette" motel rooms. Most household ranges are 30 or 36 inches wide, although 24-inch-wide units are often installed where space is limited.

Some stand-alone ranges either slip into a space between cabinets, or drop into a space that features a base which is part of the adjacent cabinets. Many have adjustable filler panels on the sides to fill any gaps and give these ranges a custom, built-in look.

The Eye-Level Range

Figure 10-1 is a freestanding eye-level range. This one has its own exhaust system and a lighted back panel. The upper oven can be a microwave. Both burner and

Figure 10-1
A freestanding eye-level range that fits snugly between cabinets

oven arrangements and special features vary from one manufacturer to another. For example, induction ranges use a technology in which the range surface never gets hot – only the utensil and its contents.

Be very careful if you're tempted to install a range at a corner next to a bank of drawers. Figure 10-

2 A shows what can happen. Even if the range itself is only 24 inches deep, the door handles (and possibly the oven door) will extend into the room so the drawers can't open in the cabinet on the other side of the corner. You'd have to use a smaller drawer base, with a filler to the corner (Figure 10-2 B).

Remember that when you remodel an older kitchen, you may have to provide additional electrical circuits to handle new appliances. Avoid connecting multiple high-demand appliances to the same circuit if they'll be running at the same time.

Cooktops

Both gas and electric cooktops come in a variety of sizes, finishes and colors. They may have as few as two or as many as eight burners. They may contain a grill, a griddle, or one or more convertible deep well cookers. Electric models come with the familiar exposed heating element, or may have a solid glass or ceramic top with the heat source beneath it. Gas models often have enameled cast iron or steel grates which may or may not incorporate a burner cover. Some have sealed burner units which prevent spills from getting under the cooktop.

Electric cooktops are usually only about 3 inches deep, so there's room for a shallow drawer under them. It's possible to build a custom drawer under the deeper gas cooktop as well. That's described in Chapter 4.

A Oven handle blocks drawer

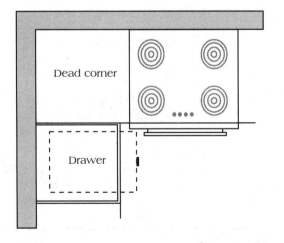

B Use a filler to prevent the problem

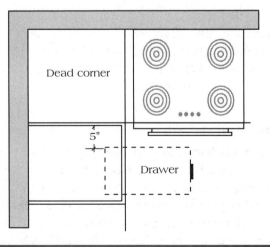

Figure 10-2
Measure carefully when you install a range next to a corner

Remember that every cooktop needs counter space on both left and right. Never install a cooktop in a corner next to a sink.

Magnetic Induction Cooktops   The heating element in this type of cooktop produces a magnetic field which causes steel, porcelain-clad steel or cast iron to get hot. The cooktop surface is Ceran®. These units heat quickly to bring foods to a boil, and are easily controlled for simmering. An indicator light shows on the control panel as long as the element remains hot.

Ceran glass-ceramic cooktops contain high-speed radiant elements and quartz halogen lamps and a black glass surface. This type of cooktop requires utensils with perfectly flat bottoms to work most efficiently. Temperature limiters keep the cooktop panel from overheating so dry or empty cookware won't melt and damage the cooktop surface.

Down-Draft Cooktops   Every cooktop requires some type of exhaust system. Newer ranges come with a built-in exhaust system which draws steam, smoke and cooking fumes down through the cooktop where they're ducted outside. Figure 10-3 A shows such a system installed against a wall, where it's vented to the roof. Figure 10-3 B shows a down-draft unit installed in an island or peninsula. In this case, the outlet is routed through the floor to the outside, or up through a wall to the roof.

If the kitchen is on a slab, without a basement or crawl space, you can run the duct and wiring under the cabinet in the toe space area. Or, you can cut a channel in the slab for the duct. You can install the wiring in the same channel if you use armored cable.

Where the down-draft unit is in a peninsula, you can route the duct to the outside wall where the peninsula is anchored. Venting for these units is described in more detail later in this chapter.

Indoor Barbecues

Indoor gas barbecue grills (see Figure 10-4) fit into a standard 24-inch-wide base cabinet. You can also put them in a 30-inch base. Be sure to plan for the gas line when your design includes a barbecue. These units are attractive when they're installed in a brick surround. Treat the brick with a product such as Thoroseal to prevent grease and spatters from discoloring or staining the brick.

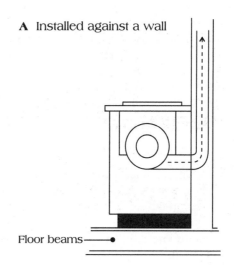

A Installed against a wall

Floor beams

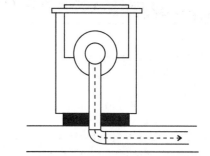

B Installed in an island or peninsula

Figure 10-3
Down-draft cooktops vented to the roof, or through the floor

Figure 10-4
An indoor gas barbecue can be used in all kinds of weather

Wall Ovens

If you use a cooktop, you also need an oven somewhere else. It's not absolutely necessary that these be right next to one another, but most people expect it. In a narrow kitchen, avoid placing the wall oven next to the kitchen entrance or opposite the dishwasher. The oven door would be an inconvenience, if not a hazard, in both situations.

Wall ovens come in about as many variations as cooktops do. You can get single oven-broiler combinations, or double ovens where one also serves as a broiler. You can combine conventional ovens, convection ovens, microwaves, warming ovens, and multipurpose ovens just about any way your customer's cooking habits demand.

Be sure to check the manufacturer's specs before you quote a price for cabinets and installation of wall ovens – some may require special ventilation. For instance, Thermador wall ovens require outside venting.

If you must vent an oven that's to be enclosed in brick, you'll have to leave an access panel like the one in Figure 10-5. That's because you need a way to connect the oven's ventilation outlet to a duct which leads outside. That connection must not leak, so it has to be taped securely. You need an access door to do that.

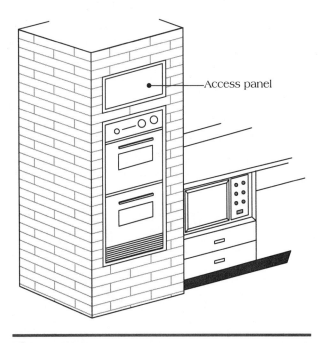

Figure 10-5
Provide access to ducting when a brick-enclosed wall oven requires ventilation

You can dress up the access door by installing a clock in it, or face it with tile to match the countertop.

Also notice in Figure 10-5 that a microwave oven is installed under the counter. The oven is still high enough to use easily, and has plenty of counter space just above it. You'd probably want to recommend some sort of heat-resistant counter saver in that situation, unless the counter is tile.

Exhaust Fans – With or Without Hoods

Every built-in cooking appliance needs exhaust ventilation to remove steam, fumes and grease from the cooking area. Kitchen exhaust fan systems vary in size and power, depending on specific requirements. Fans are rated by their capacity to exchange air in cubic feet per minute (CFM).

Measuring Exhaust Fan Capacity and Requirements

An exhaust fan should be able to circulate the air in the room or area it services about 15 times per hour. That's once every four minutes. The formula is:

Fan capacity = area volume ÷ time in minutes
for each air change

For example, in a room 10 feet wide by 15 feet long by 8 feet high, you'd need a fan rated at 300 CFM (1200 cubic feet divided by 4 minutes). The CFM rating is usually shown on a metal data plate attached to the fan.

Fan capacity in a range hood isn't always based on the size of the room. The size of the hood itself may be more important. Fan capacity should be at least 100 CFM for each linear foot of hood length. When used over peninsulas and center islands, fan capacity should be at least 120 CFM for each foot of hood length.

Using that formula, a hood 30 inches long that's mounted against a wall requires a 250 CFM fan. A 4-foot hood over an island requires at least a 480 CFM fan. Notice however, that this formula may not be adequate if the room containing the island is very large or drafty. Always check manufacturer's specs for the situation you're designing.

The hood over a cooking appliance set against a wall should be at least 20 inches above the cooking surface. If your customer is tall, mount the hood 24 inches or more above the cooktop. Otherwise that per-

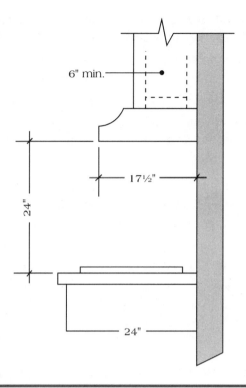

Figure 10-6
A typical hood installation over a cooktop installed
against a wall

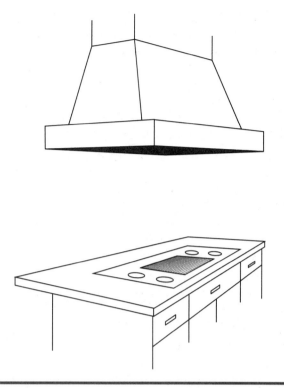

Figure 10-7
A ceiling-mounted hood above an island cooktop

son would have to bend down to see what's cooking
on the back burners. The hood should project least 17
inches from the wall. See Figure 10-6.

When a hood is over an island or peninsula, the
hood should be mounted about 30 inches above the
cooktop (more for tall users). This type of hood usually extends over the entire range or cooktop.
Remember, however, that the higher the hood, the
more powerful the fan must be. If the fan doesn't
draw enough air, cooking fumes will rise around the
hood, not into it.

Figure 10-7 shows a typical hood arrangement
over an island cooktop.

A hood with square corners is a hazard in any
kitchen. There's real danger in bumped heads on
sharp corners. Figure 10-8 illustrates a design which
minimizes that hazard. Besides being safer, it's a
more graceful-looking unit.

In older kitchens, a simple kitchen fan was often
installed in a ceiling duct. Unless the fan was very
powerful, it had little effect because of its distance
from the cooking surface. A better location, if you

must use this type of fan, would be the backsplash
behind the cooktop, as shown in Figure 10-9.

Excess fan capacity is no advantage. Turning on
the fan shouldn't create a tornado that snuffs out pilot
lights on the range. Provide enough capacity and use
a variable-speed fan so the user can decide how much
air movement is needed.

The Ductless Hood Exhaust System

These units are ideal for apartments or small con-
dos where venting to the outside is impractical and

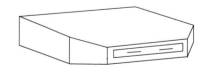

Figure 10-8
Use a hood with angled corners for safety and a
more streamlined look

Figure 10-9
The most basic exhaust fan works better when it's mounted on the wall

you have to hold costs down. One brand, Air-O Hood, comes in widths from 24 to 48 inches. They're available from:

Universal Metal Industries
48 North 56th Street
Phoenix, AZ 85034

The ductless models feature a two-speed motor which exceeds FHA requirements for cool and quiet operation. The unit contains a lifetime aluminum filter plus a replaceable activated charcoal filter to capture airborne smoke, odors and grease. It also has a light that's easy to clean and replace. Figure 10-10 illustrates a typical ductless hood system.

Cluster Blowers and Axial-Flow Fans

These are a good choice over two adjacent cooking surfaces on an island or a peninsula. A stamped disc with three or more blades moves the air. In axial-flow fans, the air flows straight through an impeller mounted within a close-fitting tube. The mixed flow impeller is like a propeller at intake, and like a blower at discharge.

Centrifugal Pressure Fans

Another exhaust system features a centrifugal fan mounted over the cooking surface. The force of the revolving squirrel-cage fan pressurizes the air passing through the blower and turns the vaporized grease back into liquid form. The liquid collects inside a fire-safe blower housing which can be removed and washed in the kitchen sink. These blowers are very effective at removing all cooking by-products. They're safer than grease filters, and they're easier to clean. One of the best known and most frequently-used systems of this type is the Vent-A-Hood, with its "Magic Lung" exhauster. You can contact them at P.O. Box 830426, Richardson, TX, 75083, telephone 214-235-5201. I especially recommend these for islands and peninsulas. They're 50 percent more efficient than conventional mesh filter exhausters. For example, the Magic Lung rated at 600 CFM provides the same ventilation as a conventional unit rated at 900 CFM.

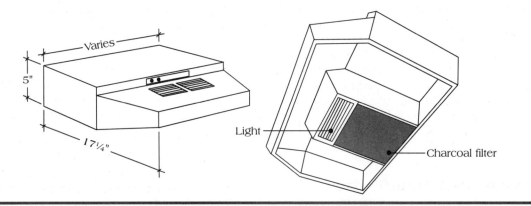

Figure 10-10
An exhaust hood that doesn't need a duct

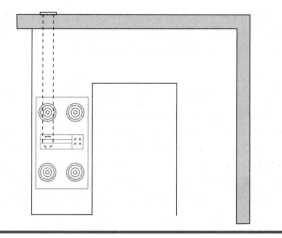
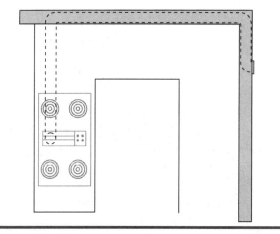

Figure 10-11
Down-draft ducting is easy through a peninsula that butts an outside wall

Figure 10-12
This duct must cross to the opposite side of the room

Down-Draft Systems

Some cooktops come with a ventilation system built in. One type has an opening in the horizontal surface of the cooktop, with a fan beneath, to draw fumes in and duct them outside. Other manufacturers use a panel across the back of the cooktop. The panel either tilts up from the cooking surface, or rises vertically. In either case, raising the panel turns on a fan within. When the fan isn't in use, the panel recedes back into the cooktop, out of the way.

Venting an Exhaust Fan

When the cooking appliance is set against a wall, an overhead exhaust fan is usually vented through the wall, or through an upper cabinet, and on up through the attic to the roof.

Duct converters are connecting pieces used to turn corners with ducting or change from round to oblong ducting. Oblong ducting is required when round ducts won't fit inside a wall or crawl space. Then oval ducting of the required capacity has to be attached to round duct. Converters tend to decrease duct capacity. That reduces the effective capacity of the exhaust fan. Be sure to use a fan with enough power to propel the vented air through a constricted duct system. And never use ducting smaller than that recommended by the fan manufacturer.

Venting a Down-Draft Exhaust

Down-draft venting is more complicated. I recommend following the manufacturer's instructions to the letter. Be sure to find the most direct route for the exhaust duct. Otherwise cooking fumes and odors may accumulate and make the kitchen unpleasant at meal times.

One installer I know had a job that required a down-draft range vent. The home had a full basement, so he planned to run the ducting through the basement. But when it was time to install the duct, he found a large beam under the floor where the duct had to run. To get around it, he used 4-inch duct instead of 6-inch duct as recommended by the manufacturer. When the customer turned the fan on for the first time, the exhaust worked for about two seconds, then shot everything back into the room. That's because 6-inch duct has over twice the capacity of 4-inch duct. There's a lesson in this story: Never deviate from the manufacturer's directions.

The way you lead duct out of the building is equally important. Every change of direction reduces the effectiveness of the fan. If you can't reach the outside with less than four bends or elbows, don't try to install a down-draft unit.

Figure 10-11 shows the ideal duct run through a peninsula. There's a straight shot from the cooktop to the outside wall. In new construction, plan the exact place where the duct will emerge through the outside wall. That makes it unnecessary to break through later.

Unfortunately, duct runs aren't always that easy. In Figure 10-12, the end wall is an interior wall, and there's no crawl space or basement. The studs in the end wall have to be headered, as shown in Figure 10-13, so the duct can pass through the base of the wall to the outside. Ideally, this should be done when the building is under construction.

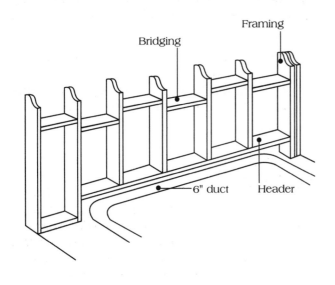

Bridging

Framing

6" duct   Header

Figure 10-13
You may need to header a stud wall to make room for a duct

Refrigeration Equipment

At the beginning of this book we discussed the Basic Rules of kitchen design and how important the refrigerator's location is to good kitchen design and function. The refrigerator is the busiest kitchen appliance, used at meal preparation time and countless times during the day for snacks or beverages. It must be convenient to the sink, and of course, have an adjacent, roomy countertop. Now, let's discuss features and installation details for refrigerators.

Today's household refrigerators come in all sizes, from the under-counter mini-fridge to the double-wide refrigerator-freezer combination. Some have exposed condensing coils on the back of the unit. In others, the coils are enclosed.

Newer models are "front breathing." That is, heat from the motor escapes through a vent at the bottom front of the unit. These can be enclosed, with upper cabinets extending all the way down to the top of the refrigerator. Older units require at least 3 inches of space above for free circulation of air. Without it, the condenser motor will burn out.

Every refrigerator manufacturer stresses features they believe sets their product apart from the competition. But most share common attributes such as reversible doors, climate control to prevent condensation outside the box, and adjustable shelves.

Freestanding refrigerators are often placed so there's a small space at the back and on one or both sides where small objects or spills collect. A broom handle is useful to retrieve items or clean up a spill. But sometimes you have to pull the refrigerator out from the wall. That's not easy, even when the refrigerator is on casters.

One way to avoid that problem is to build a cabinet around the refrigerator. See Figure 10-14. Leave just enough clearance on both sides of the refrigerator so it can be moved out for repair or replacement. Just <$E3/4> inch on each side is enough. Unless the refrigerator vents from the front, remember you have to leave at least 3 inches of clearance on top, also.

Put removable vertical dividers in the cabinet above the refrigerator. That makes useful storage space for flat items like trays, cookie sheets and shallow baking pans. Make the dividers removable so anything too wide to fit upright between the dividers can fit at an angle with a divider removed. This cabinet arrangement gives a conventional refrigerator the appearance of a more expensive built-in model.

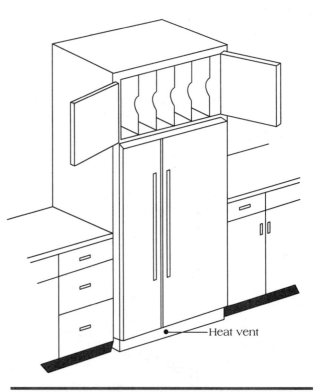

Heat vent

Figure 10-14
An enclosed refrigerator eliminates troublesome small spaces

Allow for a New Refrigerator in the Future

Some of your clients won't want to buy a new refrigerator immediately. In that case, you have to design the cabinets to accommodate the future refrigerator. In Figure 10-15 the existing small fridge sat beneath a wide, set-back upper cabinet. That's common in older kitchens. The new refrigerator was to be 6 inches wider and 8 inches taller than the existing one.

This came up in a job my company took on. Our design included an enclosure sized for the new refrigerator. But we wanted to avoid the awkward gaps that would exist until the old refrigerator was replaced. We solved the problem by building a temporary front for the lower part of the new refrigerator cabinet. See Figure 10-16 A. The vent grille allows heat to escape above the existing refrigerator. We'll remove it, along with the filler strips on the sides, when the new refrigerator is installed. Figure 10-16 B shows the new refrigerator in place.

Specialized Refrigeration Units

For a client with a large family or who entertains a lot, your design might include an under-counter refrigerator with ice-maker like the one in Figure 10-

17. The unit is only 28¼ inches high by 21 inches wide by 23 inches deep. It can make up to a thousand ice cubes a day.

I've also recommended an under-counter wine cabinet as in Figure 10-18. These units maintain recommended temperatures for wine in up to three zones between 45 and 60 degrees F, and also control humidity.

Dishwashers

The dishwasher is almost as universal in today's kitchen as a refrigerator. Most homeowners wouldn't dream of being without one. Even the most compact kitchen can accommodate a small, 18-inch-wide dishwasher. The pre-wash cycle and disposal feature available on today's dishwashers make hand rinsing virtually unnecessary.

Trim kits let you install dishwashers to blend or match perfectly with the surrounding cabinets. But even though the dishwasher is attractive enough to be installed anywhere in the kitchen, correct location is still important.

It matters little whether the dishwasher is to the right or the left of the sink. That's strictly a matter of

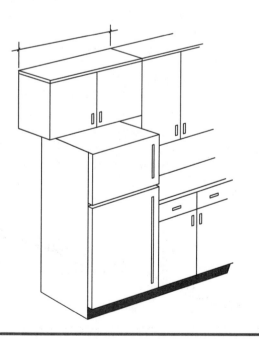

Figure 10-15
Here's room for a larger refrigerator where a small one stands now

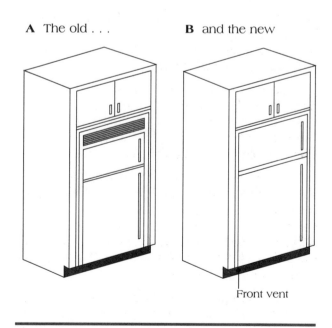

A The old . . .   **B** and the new

Front vent

Figure 10-16
Cabinet with false front holds the small refrigerator now, but leaves room for a larger one

Figure 10-17
An under-counter refrigerator with an ice-maker

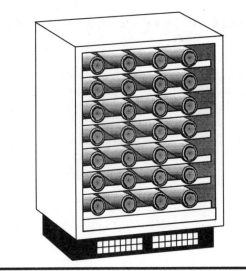

Figure 10-18
A cabinet designed to keep wine at its best

your client's personal preference. But never place a dishwasher at right angles to the sink. You won't have access to the sink with the dishwasher door open. When you install a dishwasher next to a sink set diagonally at a corner, use at least a 5-inch filler between the two to allow standing room for the user.

Trash and Garbage Handling

Trash compactors crunch household garbage into a compact bundle that takes less room in your trash can on pickup day. It also reduces the volume of material deposited at landfills. But they do use energy, and they're not entirely trouble-free. An economical alternative, which takes the same 12- to 18-inch-wide under-counter space, is the built-in trash bin. It doesn't take up floor space, and the face of the bin can match the rest of the cabinets.

One word of caution about locating the compactor or trash bin: Don't put it immediately next to the sink. That space is better used for a drawer cabinet to contain silverware and towels.

Garbage Disposals

Garbage disposals can be installed under any sink. But probably the best location is in a separate well apart from the main sink. There's less danger of dropping silverware and other small objects in a disposal that's in a separate sink well.

In Summary

Part of the pleasure of every newly-remodeled kitchen is fresh, new, clean appliances. But anyone can buy and install a few new appliances. Your help isn't needed at all. What you can do is help the owners select modern appliances that meet their needs exactly – and then plan installation of those appliances so each becomes a convenience and source of pleasure for many years.

Test Questions for Chapter 10

1. What are the standard sizes for freestanding ranges?

2. Electric cooktops are only about 3 inches deep. Why is that an advantage?

3. When a cooktop is set into an island or a peninsula, how can you vent it without installing an exhaust hood above?

4. How many times per hour should a kitchen exhaust system be able to circulate the room air?

5. What is the minimum fan capacity per linear foot of hood length for a wall-mounted exhaust fan?

6. What should the fan capacity be for an exhaust fan over an island or peninsula?

7. What is the recommended distance from the counter to the bottom of a wall-mounted exhaust hood?

8. When you install a freestanding refrigerator between two base cabinets, why is it a good idea to eliminate the small spaces between the refrigerator and the cabinets, and how can you do it?

9. Why shouldn't you place a dishwasher at right angles to the sink?

10. What are the advantages of a trash bin instead of a trash compactor?

CHAPTER 11

Small Appliances & Special Kitchen Features

Many cooks appreciate having their favorite, most-used appliances built into kitchen work spaces. That way, those appliances are always conveniently available. And built-ins often free up counter space that would be taken up by their portable equivalents.

Built-in Appliances

We'll look at four of the most popular built-in appliances: can openers, toasters, blenders and food processors, and the combination food center.

Can Openers

When you install a recessed can opener on the backsplash behind a kitchen counter, be sure to mount it high enough so the user can open tall cans like those for coffee or shortening. Some can openers can be installed on the underside of the upper cabinet.

Toasters

The toaster is one small appliance that homemakers usually leave out all the time. It's used so often that dragging it out and putting it away again every time it's needed can be a nuisance. A toaster that's recessed into the wall adds significantly more useable counter space.

Several companies make recessed toasters. One type like the one in Figure 11-1 A pulls straight out from the wall like a drawer. It's available from Iron-A-Way®, 220 W. Jackson, Morton, IL 61550. Others tilt open at an angle. Figure 11-1 B shows one of these.

Most recessed toasters require a space of at least 14 inches wide by about 11 inches high. You can install them in a wall between standard 2 x 4 studs. The toaster housing only protrudes about 2 inches from the wall when it's stored.

Blenders and Food Processors

A kitchen with too little counter space can be more than cluttered when the cook needs to use the mixer, blender, and food processor. Many people just leave these

A Slide-out toaster in masonry wall

B Tilt-out toaster in stud wall

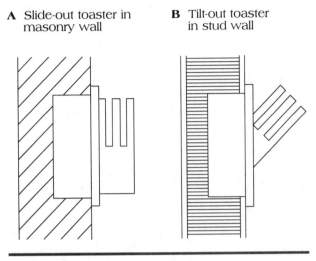

Figure 11-1
Toasters can be recessed into the wall

The Appliance Garage

I've found that people who love to cook usually like small cooking appliances. They have machines to dice, chop, juice, shred, blend, mix, knead, brew, seal, sharpen, and grind. But few have enough counter space to keep all these gadgets close at hand. The appliance garage was invented for these folks.

These small enclosures fill the space between the upper cabinets and the countertop. National Products Inc. of Louisville, Kentucky makes ready-to-install and custom tambour door kits. Some are designed to go under a corner diagonal wall cabinet, or you can install rectangular appliance garages, up to 3 feet long, beneath a straight run of upper cabinets. Roll-up tambour doors are convenient for appliance garages because the appliances slide right out. They don't have to be lifted off a shelf or over a cabinet door frame.

out, taking up valuable space. But at least one company has created a solution to this problem.

The Nutone Food Center

This machine's base is installed flush in the countertop. You can store the components and accessories in any convenient cabinet or drawer. The base unit measures about 5¼ inches wide by 11 inches long so there's room for a small drawer next to it. You can supply whatever accessories your client wants. They can add others later. These appliances are readily accessible at all times without adding to kitchen clutter. Figure 11-2 shows two perspectives of the Nutone unit recessed in a counter, combined with a drawer as part of a standard base cabinet.

Retractable Appliance Shelves

Heavy or cumbersome kitchen appliances, such as a stand mixer, can be stored on a shelf which swings up and out of a base cabinet. The shelf is attached to two steel brackets fastened to the top of the cabinet interior. When in use, the shelf, with appliance, lifts smoothly out and up from the cabinet, locking into place level with the countertop. One type of lift-up shelf mechanism is available from H. A. Fele American Co., PO Box 4000, Archdale, NC 27263.

The shelf has two advantages. It saves lifting a heavy and awkward appliance out of the cabinet.

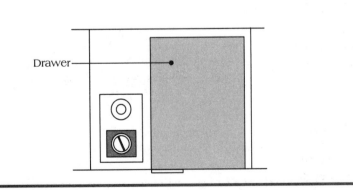

Drawer

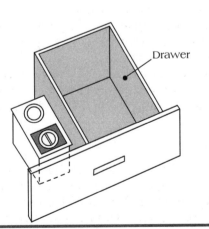

Drawer

Figure 11-2
The Nutone Food Center base rests flush with the countertop

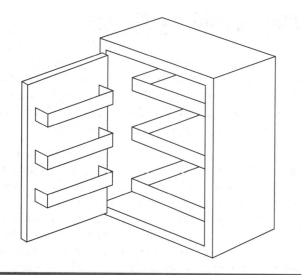

Figure 11-3
A shallow cabinet is ideal for spices

Second, in use, it supplies its own counter space. The appliance doesn't have to be fastened to the shelf because the shelf remains level as it's raised and lowered. The shelf unlocks with light finger pressure and swings back down into the cabinet after use. Steel springs counterbalance the weight of the appliance, and can be adjusted to hold from 6 to 30 pounds.

Hide-A-Shelf is a similar CabinetAides system. It can be mounted in any cabinet with an inside height of at least 22½ inches. The shelf itself isn't included with either of these units. Cut a shelf to fit the installed brackets.

Special Storage Units

Many of the items commonly used in a kitchen have an unusual shape that requires a customized space for storage. These custom-designed spaces can make your kitchens stand out – and build your reputation as a clever and creative designer. Best of all, this storage space is a low-cost luxury most homeowners can afford.

Spices

Spices, like fine wines, are fussy about where they're stored. Quality often deteriorates noticeably when they're exposed to excessive heat or extreme humidity or dryness. Because most spices come in small containers, you waste a lot of space if you store them on a standard cabinet shelf. And if you stack

them, it's always the one on the bottom of the stack that you want. They really need a home of their own.

There are all kinds of useful and decorative spice racks available in stores. Your customers can buy those, and mount them anywhere on a wall or inside a cabinet door. But you, as kitchen designer, can use your imagination and build spice storage into your kitchen designs.

If there's a spot where you can't use a cabinet of standard depth because of space restrictions or an obstruction along a wall, build a spice cabinet instead. A cabinet only 7 inches deep is enough for spice cans or jars arranged in single rows. Place shelves 5 to 6 inches apart in the cabinet and on the cabinet door. You can even make those shelves adjustable. Just be sure to put a lip or retainer on the door shelves to keep the contents from toppling off. Figure 11-3 shows a handy spice cabinet. This cabinet can be any height and width to fit the space available.

Figure 11-4 is another solution when a kitchen has plenty of drawer space. Outfit the drawer with dividers shaped something like a concrete grandstand. All the containers (and their labels) will be easy to see and reach.

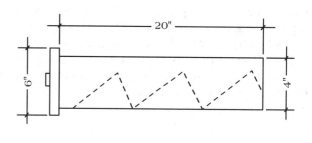

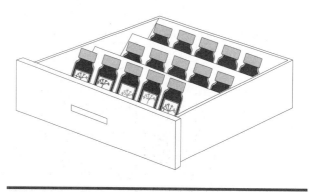

Figure 11-4
Here's a drawer outfitted to hold spice bottles

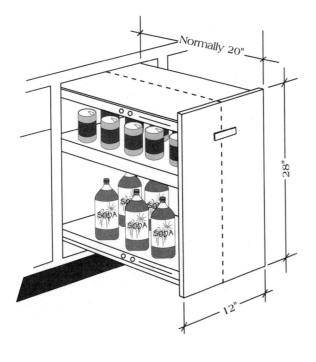

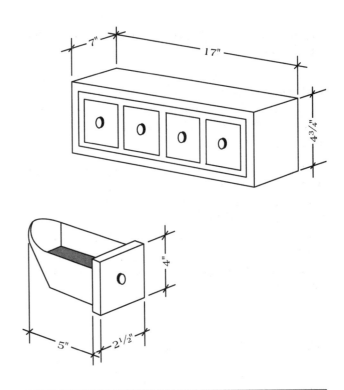

Figure 11-5
A pull-out shelf unit holds beverage cans and bottles

Figure 11-6
Handy storage for baking needs, pasta or grains

Cutlery

Divided cutlery drawers are especially convenient when they're near the cutting board or cooktop. In Chapter 5, we described a partitioned drawer that can be installed at the top of the base cabinet under a cooktop. Even a shallow partitioned drawer provides a handy place for knives, spatulas, and other long, flat utensils. Never waste the space under the cooktop; it's perfect for this type of storage.

Knape & Vogt, PO Box 946, La Mirada, CA 90638 makes a knife rack that mounts beneath an upper cabinet and folds away out of sight when not in use. (They also make a similar unit to hold a cookbook.)

Soda Cans and Bottle Storage

If you have a space for an extra 12- to 15-inch-wide base cabinet, turn it into beverage storage cabinet. Figure 11-5 illustrates a pull-out suspension storage unit with a divider in the center that lets you store cans or bottles on both sides. Use heavy-duty tracks to support this unit. Otherwise the weight will tend to jam the tracks.

Baking Needs or Grains

Figure 11-6 shows a storage unit with separate scoop-shaped compartments to hold such things as noodles, grains, or baking ingredients. You can mount a unit like this on the wall, or under an upper cabinet. These also come in a two-tiered model.

Tablecloths

The normally dead corner at the end of a peninsula is an ideal place for a cabinet like the one in Figure 11-7. Fresh tablecloths hang on slide-out racks where they're handy to the breakfast or dining area. Knape & Vogt makes sliding bar units for this purpose. Install a drawer over the tablecloth slides to hold extra silverware or serving pieces, napkins and napkin rings, or place mats. This is an ideal way to use an otherwise dead corner.

Garden Windows

For those who love plants and flowers, the kitchen is the perfect place for an easy-to-install garden window, as shown in Figure 11-8. In many homes, the humidity and light in the rest of the house may be too low for plants to thrive, but the kitchen usually has plenty of both.

These windows come in sizes to fit most standard-sized window openings. They have a vent which can be opened to admit fresh air in mild weather. Otherwise, it's securely closed. Sturdy wire shelves support potted plants.

Garden windows project about 8 inches outside the building and have adjustable shelves. These windows are available through building supply companies, from many different manufacturers. They can be installed in place of conventional windows in all kinds of construction. Just be sure they're high enough and away from play areas so kids don't hit their heads on the corners.

Warmer Drawers

At least one manufacturer (Thermador) still makes a warmer drawer. These were once very popular. They're designed to keep food fresh and moist at a temperature of from 140 to 210 degrees for as long as four hours after cooking. The drawer takes up about 12 inches of vertical space when built into a 24-inch-wide base cabinet, so there's room for two roll-out shelves beneath it. The drawer itself is divided into compartments to hold different types of food.

Today, microwave ovens are built into nearly every modern kitchen. So, when you can warm food in 20 seconds, why keep food warm in a tray? For the cook who prepares a variety of foods, and needs to have them ready to serve at unpredictable times, the warmer drawer still has its place.

Today's homeowners enjoy kitchens that are light, airy, efficient and spacious. Unfortunately they're not always as spacious as they'd like. That's why it's important to build in lots of space-saving and convenient features when designing or remodeling a kitchen. The tips in this chapter should help you do that.

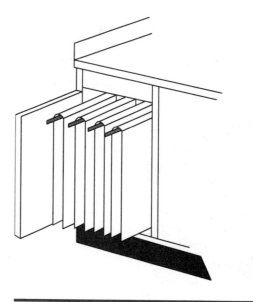

Figure 11-7
Here's a cabinet custom-designed for tablecloth storage

Figure 11-8
A garden window brings the outdoors in

Test Questions for Chapter 11

1. What are the benefits of installing built-in small appliances, such as toasters and can openers?

2. What should you remember when locating a recessed can opener on the backsplash behind the countertop?

3. Since a food center base is only about $5\frac{1}{4}$ inches wide, what is a good method of installation that also provides a convenient place to store the machine's accessories?

4. What is the best way to provide storage for a heavy food mixer?

5. Name two ways to store spices, while keeping them within easy reach.

6. Describe a convenient place to store soda cans and bottles in the kitchen.

7. How can grains and baking needs be stored conveniently?

8. When a kitchen has an electric cooktop, there is often space under it. What can this be used for?

9. What is an ideal use for the dead corner at the end of a peninsula?

10. What is the hidden danger to watch for when selecting where to install a garden window?

CHAPTER 12
Kitchen Floors

Today kitchen designers can choose from a wide variety of durable and attractive floor finish materials. That wasn't true a hundred years ago. Back then, random hardwood flooring planks nailed to sleepers were the most common finish flooring in kitchens. Usually the boards were uneven, poorly matched and left unfinished. Later, plank flooring was protected with varnish or shellac. As better milling equipment was developed, wood flooring also improved. Floor plank was closely matched and milled for tongue-and-groove construction. The boards were securely fastened with deeply countersunk nails or screws. Fastener holes were filled with hardwood pegs. Even today, some of the highest quality, most desirable kitchen floor finishes are made to resemble those pegged wood floors.

Over the years, linoleum became the surface of choice for kitchen floors, and even countertops. Linoleum was a major improvement over most plank flooring. It was durable, nonporous, could be cleaned with soap and water and waxed to a high gloss. It came in a range of colors and patterns, and was available in wide rolls, which permitted seamless installation in all but the largest rooms.

Today's vinyl flooring far outlasts linoleum and is available with a no-wax finish that remains bright and shiny with a minimum of upkeep. Manufacturers offer an endless array of patterns and designs that give the appearance of anything from cobblestones to glass chips to brick or even wood. Vinyl comes in rolls 6 and 12 feet wide for seamless installation, and is also available as self-stick 8- and 12-inch square tiles which are easy to cut and lay by the do-it-yourselfer.

Flooring Materials

The subfloor is the structural base for the floor, whether it's sheathing or concrete. Underlayment goes down over the subfloor and is covered by the finish flooring.

Underlayment Materials

Several type of material can be used for underlayment. The purpose of underlay is to create a smooth, even surface that provides solid support for the finish

flooring material. Materials commonly used for underlay include:

Oriented strand board and *flakeboards*, sometimes known as *waferboards*. These are made of pressed wood fiber bonded into a smooth, dense sheet. They have little structural strength but are dense enough to resist compression under foot traffic.

Plywood is composed of three to five layers of wood, each laid with the grain at a right angle to the grain above or below. Plywood is suitable for underlayment if it's $^7/_{16}$ inch or thicker and won't be exposed to the weather.

Hardboard or *Masonite* provides a smooth, hard surface and is probably the cheapest form of underlayment.

Use any of these materials to cover old, single-layer, 3-inch-wide or less strip wood floors before you cover the floor with vinyl or tile.

When you install underlayment, make sure all holes are patched so the finish floor can be laid on a smooth surface. Any bumps, even those which aren't readily visible, will be felt under a resilient floor, will be apparent under certain lighting conditions, and can cause hardwood or tile to be uneven.

Finish Materials

Brick or Stone   To install brick or stone floors, first fasten waterproofed tarpaper to the underlayment or existing floor. Then lay a coat of portland cement mortar reinforced with 16 gauge wire mesh. Fasten the brick with a thin coat of epoxy mortar bond coat. Leave $^1/_2$-inch spaces between the brick for the mortar joints.

Use a 2" x 2" x 8" rubber sponge to fill the joints with C-Cured grout, sometimes called Thinset. This grout material comes in a variety of colors to blend or contrast with the brick. To clean off mortar stains, use SureKlean or a mild solution of $^1/_4$ pail of muriatic acid to a full pail of water applied with a "Tampico" fiber brush. Use a Carborundum stone with the cleaning solution on stubborn stains.

Brick flooring is generally finished with several coats of a waterproof material such as Thompson's Waterseal or Thoroseal to both protect and add luster to the flooring.

Carpet   Some people prefer carpeting on a kitchen floor because of its warmth and sound-deadening qualities. Carpets are comfortable under foot but have drawbacks which may make them unsuitable for use in an active kitchen. Kitchen spills must be cleaned up promptly or they'll result in a stain.

Immediately absorb spills with several layers of paper towel or white terry toweling. (Stand on the towel to soak up as much liquid as possible.) Then try spraying with plain water, again absorbing as much liquid as possible. This often works on most of today's synthetic and stain-protected carpet materials. Avoid scrubbing, but if you must use a cloth or sponge on a stain, work into the stain from the clean part of the carpet.

If plain water doesn't do the trick, use a commercial product such as Nylac or Folex, following manufacturer's directions. Or try one of the following:

♦   A solution of $^1/_8$ teaspoon of liquid dishwashing detergent to a pint of lukewarm water

♦   Non-flammable dry cleaning solvent

♦   A weak acid solution (one part white vinegar to one part water) is especially effective for cat and dog "accidents"

♦   A solution of 1 tablespoon ammonia to a cup of water

In any case, follow cleaning instructions supplied by the mill.

You also have to use extra care to avoid damage when moving heavy furniture or appliances over carpet. Use skids made from thin sheets of plywood or Masonite to protect carpet from stains, scuffs or tears.

Ceramic Tile   Even though it's cold, hard, and slippery when wet, ceramic tile is popular because of its durability and ease of maintenance. Decorators love it because it comes in so many shapes, sizes, colors and textures. Even thick Mexican tile and Spanish pavers find their way into rustic decorating schemes. However, I advise against tile with an irregular surface because it's uncomfortable to walk on. Glazed tile is easy to clean and requires no other finish or dressing of any kind.

When you replace an existing vinyl or linoleum floor with tile, the difference in floor thickness may present a problem. For instance, installing inch-thick tile in front of a dishwasher may seem like a fine idea. But wait till the unit needs to be moved for repair or replacement. Also, raising the floor an inch might press the refrigerator tight against the cabinet above. If it's already a tight fit, another inch may be an inch too much. Take careful vertical measurements when you install thick tiles.

Figure 12-1
Use a scraper like this to remove sheet flooring

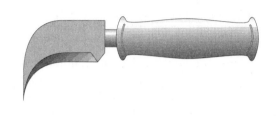

Figure 12-2
A hook or utility knife

Tile is fairly expensive compared to other floor coverings. Try to save your client some money by not laying tile under major appliances. Instead, install a waterproofed wood panel under the range, refrigerator and dishwasher. Use plywood or ¼-inch lightweight concrete board the same thickness as the tile, and cut it slightly smaller than the appliance itself. Butt the tile flush against the wooden panel so the panel doesn't show when the appliance is in place. This should work even with the dishwasher if the leveling legs can be cranked down enough to squeeze the dishwasher under the countertop.

Ceramic tile is installed much the same way as brick or stone. Lay a sheet of "Blue Membrane" over the underlayment, secured at the edges with duct tape to provide a moisture barrier and prevent condensation. Then set the tile in Thinset and fill the joints. Use a soft towel to wipe off any haze that remains.

Removing Old Floors

Beware of asbestos. Old floors of tile or sheet material, and their backings or felt linings may contain asbestos fibers. You don't want to inhale this stuff. If you suspect that asbestos felt was used in the floor, avoid creating dust when removing the old floor. Don't sand the floor or backing and don't try to scrape off the residual felt backing. Wear a mask or respirator when you demolish the floor. Place floor felt you've removed in heavy-duty impermeable trash bags or other closeable containers. If you must sweep the surface, moisten the surface with a fine mist of water or mild detergent solution before you begin.

Floor Removal Equipment

Use the following equipment to remove resilient sheet flooring:

1) Stiff-bladed wall or floor scraper (Figure 12-1)

2) Utility or hook knife (Figure 12-2)

3) Tank-type high-efficiency particulate vacuum cleaner. These cleaners are more powerful than an ordinary shop-vac and capture even the finest dust particles.

4) A solution (one ounce per gallon of water) of dishwashing detergent or wallpaper remover applied with a hand sprayer, sprinkling can or mop. Use this to loosen materials and make it safer to clean up dusty residue.

Removing Resilient Sheet Flooring

Follow these steps to remove loose or peripherally-adhered sheet flooring:

1) Remove moldings from doorways and walls and metal strips at joints with other flooring materials.

2) Cut flooring into strips about 18 inches wide. Roll the strips face out into a tight roll. Tie or tape the rolls securely. Place them in a heavy-duty impermeable trash bag or closed container large enough to accommodate several rolls for disposal.

Follow these steps to remove fully-adhered sheet flooring:

1) Remove any binding strips or moldings.

2) Make a series of parallel cuts 4 to 8 inches apart through the top layers and about halfway through the backing, parallel to the wall.

3) Start at the end of the room farthest from the entrance door and pry up a corner of a strip, separating the backing layer. Peel the cut strips from the backing by pulling or by rolling around a core which will control the stripping angle and create a uniform tension. Some resilient flooring wear layers may not strip readily and may require scraping. Afterwards, thoroughly remove the residue by vacuuming, sweeping or mopping.

Removing Resilient Tile

If an existing resilient tile floor is smooth and tightly bonded to the subfloor, lay the new floor over the old. Otherwise, you'll have to remove the existing floor. Here are the tools you'll need:

1) Heavy-duty scraper or broad chisel with about a 4-inch blade and a 6- to 8-inch handle (Figure 12-3) or a weighted, long-handled floor scraper.

2) Heavy hammer

3) Commercial hand-held hot air blower to soften adhesive for easier removal.

4) Trash bags to hold the demolished flooring

Resilient tile usually sticks the tightest where it's exposed to the most foot traffic. For that reason, begin removing tiles from areas which receive the least traffic. Try to remove each tile intact.

Begin by carefully wedging your scraper into the seam between two adjoining tiles. Gradually force the

Figure 12-3
Wide chisel or scraper

edge, then the body of the tile away from the floor. Use a twisting motion with the scraper to loosen the tile. You may have to strike the scraper handle with a hammer to loosen tiles that were spread heavily with adhesive. Wear long sleeves, long pants, and goggles or safety glasses when you do this to protect yourself from sharp, flying tile or adhesive chips.

Cleanup After Demolition

Clean the exposed underlayment with the vacuum cleaner positioned so that the exhaust air doesn't blow over the uncleaned area and raise dust. Also, don't dry-sweep. Mist the area lightly with water to keep the dust down. If any floor covering including backing or adhesive remains stuck to the floor, remove it by scraping after first applying enough water to loosen the adhesive.

Installing Floors

Don't begin installing any new floor until the surface you're installing it over is perfectly level and smooth. You can level an uneven concrete subfloor with a latex preparation available from a builder's supply that handles masonry supplies. Use the same material to fill cracks in wood underlayment. But don't use it to flood the surface over a wood subfloor. Instead, cover the old surface with smooth Masonite or hardboard.

Replacing Existing Floors

I always try to install new flooring over the existing one. Instead of removing your present resilient floor covering, go over it with your new floor. But here's a word of caution: Don't install resilient flooring over any textured material including embossed vinyl patterns. The old pattern will appear on the new floor.

If the existing floor is coming loose in spots or is uneven, you'll have to remove the old floor. Thoroughly clean and level the underlayment. Underlayment panels must be smooth and even. Any bumps or irregularities will show through the finished floor material.

Underlayment panels should not contain any substance that will stain vinyl. Examine the panels thoroughly at the lumberyard. Check for any yellowing or signs of moisture. Those may be caused by sap which might react with the new flooring or adhesive.

New resilient flooring can be installed over a single layer of old resilient flooring if the old resilient floor meets the following conditions:

1) Old flooring must not be textured or embossed

2) The old floor must be firmly bonded to the underlayment or subfloor

3) The floor must show no evidence of moisture, alkaline salts, or hydrostatic pressure (water seeping up through the floor)

4) The old floor must not be a cushion-backed material

5) The old surface must be free of wax and other finishes.

Installing Wood Floors

Climate, basement wall and subfloor construction, and the way underlayment is installed can all affect the final quality and appearance of wood flooring. This applies to resilient flooring also. Underlayment must be structurally sound and at least $1/4$ inch thick.

You might consider laying strip flooring diagonally to create a design effect or avoid having to change direction where two surfaces meet in an L- or T-shape. Diagonal installation also provides additional structural strength because it always spans the subfloor joists.

Test Questions for Chapter 12

1. What is the purpose of underlayment under the finished kitchen floor?

2. Name three types of material used for underlayment.

3. After the underlayment, what other steps must you take before installing a brick floor?

4. Why isn't carpeting a good idea in active kitchens?

5. What drawbacks are there to using ceramic tile for flooring?

6. How can you save on the amount of tile you need to cover a kitchen floor?

7. What safety precaution should you take when removing old resilient tile or sheet flooring?

8. What tools would you use to remove old resilient sheet flooring?

9. If a concrete subfloor is uneven, how can you level it?

10. What benefits are there in diagonal installation of wood flooring?

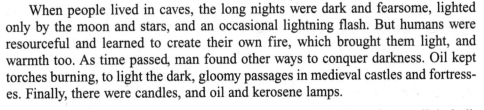

CHAPTER 13
Kitchen Lighting

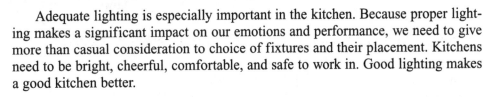

When people lived in caves, the long nights were dark and fearsome, lighted only by the moon and stars, and an occasional lightning flash. But humans were resourceful and learned to create their own fire, which brought them light, and warmth too. As time passed, man found other ways to conquer darkness. Oil kept torches burning, to light the dark, gloomy passages in medieval castles and fortresses. Finally, there were candles, and oil and kerosene lamps.

But it wasn't until Thomas Edison's genius created the incandescent light bulb that lighting set aglow every nook and cranny of the modern home. Today's lighting technology brings flexibility and control over the light in our environment to an extent undreamed of just a few decades ago.

Adequate lighting is especially important in the kitchen. Because proper lighting makes a significant impact on our emotions and performance, we need to give more than casual consideration to choice of fixtures and their placement. Kitchens need to be bright, cheerful, comfortable, and safe to work in. Good lighting makes a good kitchen better.

I grew up in a kitchen where the only light was two bare bulbs, one hanging from a cord over the sink, the other a small fixture centered over the kitchen table. Fortunately, that's well in the past. Now there are so many ways to light the kitchen that it's easy to select the most effective fixtures from the wide range of available choices.

Kitchens need both general and task lighting. General lighting should give uniform brightness throughout the room. Provide the equivalent of 175 to 200 watts of lighting for each 50 square feet of floor space. A fixture containing three 60-watt bulbs would satisfy this requirement.

If you design a luminous ceiling, provide a minimum of one 40-watt fluorescent tube for every 12 square feet of room area. This provides about 30 foot-candles of light to a surface 36 inches above the floor in a room with fairly light-colored walls. (A foot-candle is the amount of light thrown by a candle onto a square foot surface 1 foot away from the candle.)

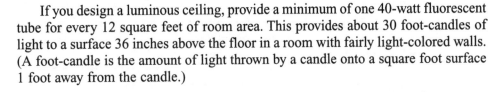

Besides the general lighting, provide task lighting over the work surfaces, range and sink. For countertop lighting, mount a 20-watt fluorescent tube beneath the cabinets for each 3 feet of counter space. In the ceiling or soffit, you can install 75-watt

24" X 24" fixture

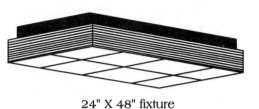

24" X 48" fixture

Figure 13-1
Typical ceiling fixtures

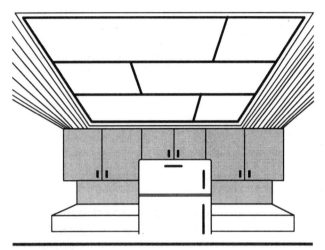

Figure 13-2
A luminous ceiling

incandescent fixtures on 24-inch centers. You can also use recessed 100-watt fixtures with built-in reflectors.

Where possible, provide for daytime lighting with skylights or "sun tubes." You can install a skylight in the same bay with recessed fluorescent ceiling lights. Install sun tubes between the attic rafters. Each tube will adequately illuminate 10 square feet of room area through a ceiling opening of only 10 inches in diameter.

Ceiling Lights

You have hundreds of good choices for ceiling lighting fixtures. There's lots of room for your clients to express their personal taste and preference. Figure 13-1 illustrates two common types of ceiling fixtures. These range in size from 2 feet square to 4 feet square. They have fluorescent tubes and can be surface mounted or recessed into the ceiling. When sur-

face mounted, they extend as little as 4 inches into the room.

The diffuser panels on these fixtures are translucent and give off a soft, non-glare and relatively shadow-free light.

The luminous ceiling in Figure 13-2 is similar to the recessed fluorescent ceiling fixture. In this case, the fluorescent fixtures are installed in a soffit or dropped ceiling. The diffusion panels become part of the ceiling.

Indirect Lighting

In kitchens with very high or cathedral ceilings, indirect lighting mounted above the cabinets or high on the wall adds to the feeling of spaciousness. Figure 13-3 shows an indirect lighting system which allows some light to shine downward through a frosted panel, as well as upward onto the wall and ceiling.

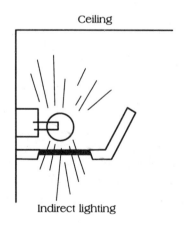

Ceiling

Indirect lighting

Figure 13-3
Indirect lighting used to wash a wall or ceiling with light

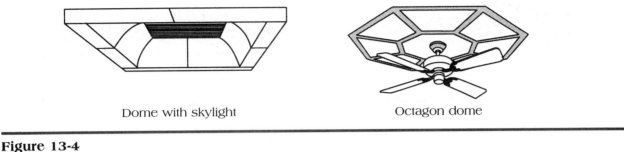

Dome with skylight | Octagon dome

Figure 13-4
Dome lighting

Dome Lighting

Where you have at least 12 inches of space above the upper cabinets for a soffit or dropped ceiling, consider installing a dome light, as shown in Figure 13-4. These can be designed in almost any shape and size, and will fit into even a narrow kitchen. These ceilings are more attractive than an ordinary flat ceiling, make the room seem more spacious, and they don't have to be painted.

Fluorescent tubes are installed around the perimeter of the fixture. Curved or slanted diffusion panels extend to the normal ceiling height. In the center, you can install a paddle fan or a bubble skylight.

Strip Lighting and Hi-Hats

Strip or track lighting lets you focus light on a particular object or section of a room. Strip lights allow greater flexibility because they can be moved and pointed to wherever the owners want additional light. Figure 13-5 shows some typical track lights.

Track systems come in 2-, 4-, 8- and 12-foot lengths so you can arrange them to suit any configuration. The modules are measured from the center of the outlet box to the center of the connector. Connectors can be live-end, straight, T- or X-shaped. Junction boxes are added separately.

You can mount them on either the wall or ceiling or hang them from standards attached to the ceiling. Variously sized and shaped lamps snap into the track at any location. A single circuit will support a track system using up to 2400 watts. The lamps are low-voltage tungsten halogen fixtures which conserve energy and produce a pure white light. Another advantage is that they last longer than ordinary bulbs. They require a tubular double contact socket capsule. You can control them with dimmer switches.

Figure 13-5
Track lighting

In new construction or major remodeling projects, hard-wire the fixtures. If that isn't possible, you can conceal the power cord in a grooved vertical surface such as a post or wall and cover it with a decorative wood molding or metal strip.

Hi-hats are recessed circular lights and come in many different styles, ranging from baffle down-lights to ellipsoidal down-lights. They come in many finishes. Some have soft color interiors. See Figure 13-6. They're always installed into a wall or ceiling rather than a track. Install their housing flush with the ceiling or soffit.

Under-Cabinet Lighting

Little Inch fixtures use fluorescent tubes and can be installed under wall cabinets. They virtually eliminate shadows and dark corners along a countertop. These fixtures range in size from 12 to 48 inches long, and are completely concealed behind a 1-inch lip on the cabinet face. At least one brand of cabinets, Poggenpohl, comes with lights like this already built in.

Use these fixtures to light the inside of cabinets over an island or peninsula. This is especially effective and pretty when the cabinet shelves and doors are made of clear or stained glass.

Figure 13-6
Recessed or "hi-hat" lighting

Conceal the wiring for these fixtures in the wall or cabinet. Under-counter fixtures have a switch on the fixture itself. Any installed out of easy reach require wiring into a box with a remote switch, or a line switch on the cord to the receptacle.

Low-Voltage Switching

Most lighting is controlled by a switch that carries the full line voltage, usually 120 volts. Low-voltage switching systems are different. While the lighting is still at 120 volts, a low-voltage switch controls a relay that turns the current to the light on and off. Low-voltage lighting is popular where many lights in a room are controlled from a single switch panel. Since the switch circuit is low voltage, wiring can be light gauge. That cuts cost. An automatic dimmer is usually built into the relay, giving the option of dimming any light on the circuit at no extra cost.

Switches and Receptacles

Install three- or four-way switches so fixtures can be turned on and off from several locations. The familiar "snap" (although most of them are silent now) or toggle switch is still commonly used. But today you're more likely to use some of the more sophisticated and attractive switches available.

Some switches can be activated by sound or pressure on a touch-sensitive panel. Others have a small pilot light in the switch handle so they're easy to find in the dark. Still others are designed to brighten or dim the fixture they control. Some have photoelectric sensors to turn lights on automatically when it gets dark. Others can only be turned on with a key. It's possible to wire switches and receptacles into a master control panel so a person can control electrical equipment all over the house from one central location.

Receptacles are just as varied, from the ordinary two-plug outlet to those which combine an electrical outlet with a telephone, TV antenna or cable jack. Some come with insulated, weatherproof caps. Others have covers built in, which prevent children from poking things into them.

The huge selection of decorative switch and outlet cover plates makes it easy to blend these fixtures with any decorating scheme or make them almost invisible against a wall or backsplash. Spend the little bit of extra effort it takes to make these accessories as attractive as possible. Your customers will appreciate it.

Wiring for the Kitchen

All outlets and switches must be grounded. And most codes today require that any switches or outlets within 4 feet of a sink, tub or shower be equipped with a GFCI (ground-fault circuit interrupter). Use 20-amp circuits for receptacles where portable appliances will be used.

Test Questions for Chapter 13

1. What kind of fixture will provide the 175 to 200 watts of lighting needed for each 50 square feet of floor space?

2. What is a foot-candle?

3. What makes a good daytime lighting system for kitchens?

4. What is an attractive type of lighting for high or cathedral ceilings?

5. How much space do you need above the upper cabinets to install dome lighting?

6. How many watts will a single circuit support in a track lighting system?

7. How would you provide good countertop lighting?

8. What are the benefits of using low-voltage switching?

9. When and why should you install three- or four-way switches?

10. What do most codes require for any switch or outlet within 4 feet of a kitchen sink?

CHAPTER 14

Decorative Kitchen Materials

Kitchens built early in the 20th century were usually isolated from the rest of the house and designed strictly for utility. Today, the kitchen is usually part of an open floor plan that may include dining space, a family room, and entertainment area. The kitchen is a much more integrated part of the home, used by family and guests – not just for cooking and eating meals.

Modern kitchens have many more decorative features than those old utilitarian kitchens. As a kitchen designer, you can choose from a wide range of materials to add warmth and beauty. There's much more to kitchen design now than bare walls, enamel-painted cabinets and white steel appliances. Of course ceramic tile is one of the most popular finishes. Or you can suggest brick or stone for a rustic look.

Tile

Decorative ceramic tile in a kitchen adds color and beauty and can be functional as well. You can install tile panels as counter savers in plastic laminate countertops, or as color accents and borders on walls and backsplashes.

For example, Figure 14-1 A shows how patterned tile dresses up an otherwise plain hood over an island cooktop. In Figure 14-1 B, tile makes the access panel over a vented wall oven more attractive.

Your imagination is the only limit to the designs you can create on custom painted tile. Figure 14-1 C is another example. I installed this cooktop wall for a customer who obviously loved the ocean. In the hands of a skilled artist, tile can be the canvas for anything from the most sophisticated to the most whimsical of designs.

Brick and Stone

Use brick or stone facing to add interest to any kitchen design. Brick makes an attractive enclosure for islands, cooktops, wall ovens, and even refrigerators. Brick facing adds warmth and texture to kitchen walls and partitions. Maybe best of all, brick is a nearly maintenance-free surface.

A Tile accents on hood cover

B Access door over wall oven

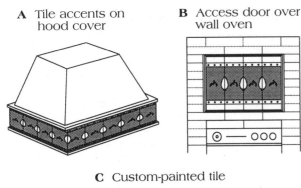

C Custom-painted tile

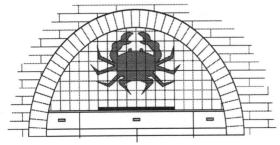

Figure 14-1
Patterned tile adds interest

Figure 14-2
A stone wall partition housing a wall oven

Stonework

You can use stone facings on walls nearly anywhere you would use brick. Figure 14-2 shows a stone wall partition which houses a wall oven in the kitchen and a fireplace in the family room on the back. The room has a high, vaulted ceiling, so the space on top of the low end of the partition is an attractive place for displaying plants or collectibles.

Supporting Masonry

Consider the weight of masonry you plan to use before drawing plans. A concrete slab will support masonry veneer, but a conventional floor over a basement or crawl space may not. When in doubt, get assistance from a licensed engineer. This isn't the place to make guesses.

Some masonry materials are much heavier than others. Granite weighs more than sandstone or brick. Solid brick is heavier than cored brick. Over a basement or crawl space, consider using lighter materials. Be sure weight is distributed evenly over floor joists. Figure 14-3 A shows how the weight of the end walls of a U-shaped enclosure bears directly on the floor, not on the supporting joists. In Figure 14-3 B, a $3/4$-inch wood panel installed under the brick enclosure helps distribute the weight evenly to the joists.

Cut the plywood panel the size and shape of the brickwork, less $1/2$ inch all around. Nail the panel securely to the flooring and the joists. Later, conceal the $1/2$-inch gap at the edges of the panel with mortar.

Choices in Masonry

Standard brick: a brick with a nominal measurement of 4 inches wide by 8 inches long by $2^1/2$ inches high. The width and length can vary by as much as $3/8$ inch. The height is fairly constant.

Jumbo brick: standard brick that's $2^3/4$ inches high

Cored brick: contains from 3 to 16 holes which run through the brick parallel to the height. The holes serve two purposes. First, they make the brick lighter so it's less expensive to ship. Second, your brickwork is more stable when you fill the holes with mortar during installation.

Joint: the mortar spaces that separate bricks from each other. Joints can be as thin as the lead in a pencil as in "buttered-joint" brickwork, or as thick as 1 inch. Most commonly, joints are between $3/8$ and $1/2$ inch thick. Keep the horizontal and vertical joints the same size. For example, if you adjust the horizontal

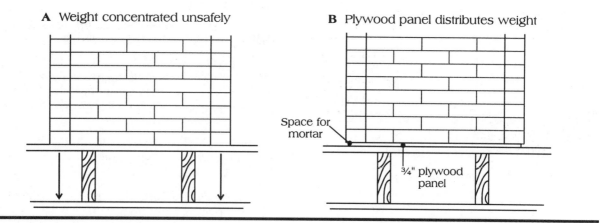

A Weight concentrated unsafely   **B** Plywood panel distributes weight

Space for mortar

¾" plywood panel

Figure 14-3
Supporting brick on a raised floor

joint (to reach a certain height), you should make the vertical joints the same thickness. Joints should border the brick like the frame around a picture. A cross joint is the vertical joint between bricks. A bed joint is the horizontal joint.

Course: a row of brick laid end to end

Stretcher: a brick laid lengthwise

Header: a brick laid perpendicular to the course below

Soldier: a brick laid upright on end

Brick Bonding Patterns

American bond: five stretcher courses and a header. The headers stabilize and bond together a wall that's two bricks thick. The header cross joint never falls directly over the stretcher joint.

Running bond: same as American bond but without headers. Wall ties or masonry reinforcing keep the wall in place.

Flemish bond: alternating stretchers and headers in each course

Dutch bond: alternating stretcher and header courses

Diamond cross bond: stretchers and headers used to form diamond shapes

The more decorative bonds are difficult to control when windows, doors or cabinets interrupt the wall. But decorative walls add interest and may be worth the extra trouble. The bonds are illustrated in Figure 14-4.

Mortar

Mortar is a mixture of sand, cement, lime and enough water to make it workable. The proportion of each material determines the mortar's durability, plasticity and strength. If you don't use enough lime, the mortar won't be plastic enough to flow into the spaces between the bricks. A mixture of 1 part portland cement, 1 part lime, and 6 parts sand makes the best mortar. It's easy to work with, and since lime is a waterproofing agent, it helps control seepage of mois-

A American bond   **B** Flemish bond   **C** Dutch bond   **D** Diamond cross bond

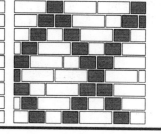

Figure 14-4
Four common brick bonds

ture. If mortar joints have to be white, use white portland cement and white sand.

On a small job, don't bother to mix mortar from scratch. The following prepared mortars are available:

Pre-mixed mortar: This is ready to use, since it contains the necessary sand, lime, and cement. All you do is add water to the proper consistency.

Super mortar: Has cement and lime in it but needs sand. This makes a good working mortar and is very popular.

Dynamor: Very plastic but somewhat slow setting. Add 3 parts sand to each part of mortar mix before using.

Sealers and Surface Treatments

Brick can develop unsightly white stains called efflorescence, caused by leaching of soluble salts in the brick. Remove these with a solution of muriatic (hydrochloric) acid. Never use the acid full strength. Follow the dilution instructions on the jug. To test the strength of the solution, let a few drops fall onto concrete or cement pavement. If there's a mild bubbling, it's an acceptable mixture. But if it turns a greenish yellow and bubbles strongly, there's too much acid. Add more water.

Protect your hands when you work with muriatic acid. Wear rubber gloves. Use a plastic bucket rather than a metal one. The acid will corrode a galvanized surface.

Brick and stone are both porous. When the backsplash behind a cooktop or grill is made of brick, spattering grease from frying food will penetrate and stain the surface. Coat the masonry with a good sealer, such as Prosoco's SureKlean or Thompson's Thoroseal to reduce absorption of liquids. The sealer both prevents staining and enhances the appearance of the brick or stone. It also prevents further efflorescence. Be sure to follow the manufacturer's directions when applying sealer.

Freestanding Brick Walls

Figure 14-5 A shows an end view of a freestanding wall that's 8 inches (two bricks) thick. A header is laid across the wall after every fifth course to add sta-

bility. You can make a wall like this as high as 25 feet without support, unless it's a bearing wall.

In Figure 14-5 B, the wall is also two bricks thick, but there's a 2-inch cavity between the bricks. There are two reasons for this space. First, it provides insulation. And second, it keeps water from leaking into the building. If water should penetrate the outer wall, it collects in the cavity, and drains back outside through a series of weep holes at the bottom of the outside wall.

This wall is stabilized by anchor rods, which prevent the two sections from pulling apart. The anchor rods fit into cored brick on every fifth course.

Attaching Brick to an Existing Wall

A 4-inch brick wall must be secured to an existing wall with corrugated metal wall ties. See Figure 14-6. Place a tie on top of every fifth course of brick, and nail the tie into a stud of the existing wall. Fasten ties to each stud with galvanized nails. Then you secure the tie to the brick with mortar and the next course of brick. You can use smooth ties, although corrugated ties hold the mortar more securely. However, corrugated ties are harder to bend.

Brick facing looks like brick but is only about ½ inch thick. You attach it to a stud wall just as you would install tile. If the backing wall is extremely slick, score it to make the mortar adhere better.

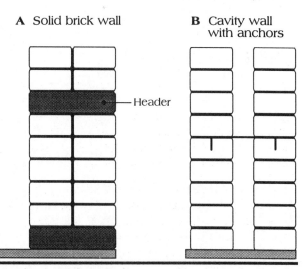

A Solid brick wall   **B** Cavity wall with anchors

— Header

Figure 14-5
Two types of brick wall

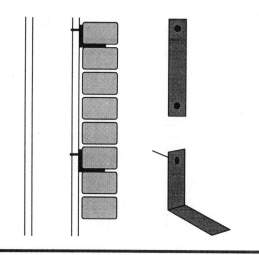

Figure 14-6
Secure face brick using wall ties

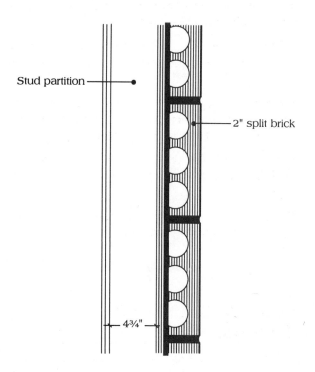

Figure 14-7
Split brick wall facing

Split Brick Facing

You can save floor space, weight and money by facing a wall with only half a brick instead of a whole brick. Just split three-hole cored brick down the center and apply it as shown in Figure 14-7. Trim off the pieces at the holes and cement them to the wall, the same as you would for tile. Use wall ties at every fifth course for stability and better adherence.

You can split the brick with a Carborundum saw or by tapping first one end, then the other, at the point where you want the brick to break. Then hit either end sharply with your hammer and the brick should break cleanly down its length. Allow for some breakage. The amount you need to allow depends on the quality of the brick and the skill of your mason.

Brick Arches

An ornamental brick arch creates an attractive alcove for a cooktop or a barbecue grill. Small arches make nice niches for showing off art objects. When planning an arched enclosure over a cooktop, mount the hood behind the arch, but high enough so it won't be visible below the crown of the arch.

If the cooktop has down-draft venting, you can put a 12-inch-deep cabinet or display shelving above the cooktop. Then install lighting inside the arch to show off the whole arrangement. See Figure 14-8. The arch has side walls that extend all the way to the front of the base cabinet. There's no room here for a large down-draft cooktop and grill under that same arch. Figure 14-8 B shows the plan view. Notice that there's not enough counter space between the enclosing arch walls. Solve the space problem by using corbels under the arch.

Figure 14-9 A shows the same size arch but with extra counter space where the arch has been tapered back toward the wall. Figure 14-9 B shows this arch in profile. I designed this arch with concrete block supports against the wall up to countertop height. That's where we laid starter brick for the arch. Each course projected 2 inches beyond the course below until the brick was flush with the base cabinets. The face of the arch was supported by the corbel-shaped side walls, and only the back 8 inches of the countertop was obstructed.

Figure 14-9 C is a front view of this arch. As you see, there's even room for a 15-inch-deep drawer under the counter in front of the concrete block support. The back wall can be either brick or tile. Finish the back wall when the side wall corbels are complete, at the point where the arch begins to turn. Tie the side wall returns into the back wall with wall ties to prevent any separation later.

A Elevation

B Plan view

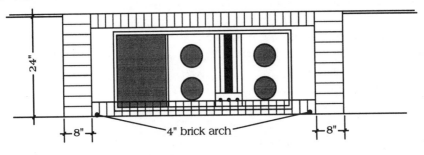

24"

8"   4" brick arch   8"

Figure 14-8
A brick arch over a cooktop

Brick Around a Diagonal Corner Wall Oven

When you set a wall oven (or any appliance) into a corner, the simplest arrangement is as shown in Figure 14-10 A. But as you can see, this arrangement wastes space in the corner and on the adjacent countertops. Figure 14-10 B shows a much better design. Make the diagonal wall 33 inches wide. Four standard bricks, and the mortar between them, total 33 inches. Then cut the cabinets on each side of the corner so they're only 16 inches deep where they meet the oven

enclosure. You gain an extra 8 inches of counter space plus upper cabinet shelf space on both sides.

Have your cabinet shop construct the angled cabinets. They can be as narrow as 15 inches, and up to 24 inches wide. If the cabinets are at least 21 inches wide, you can design them with one or more drawers.

Other Decorative Materials

Some materials not usually found in the kitchen can be used there to good advantage. And some materials formerly required for structure or function are

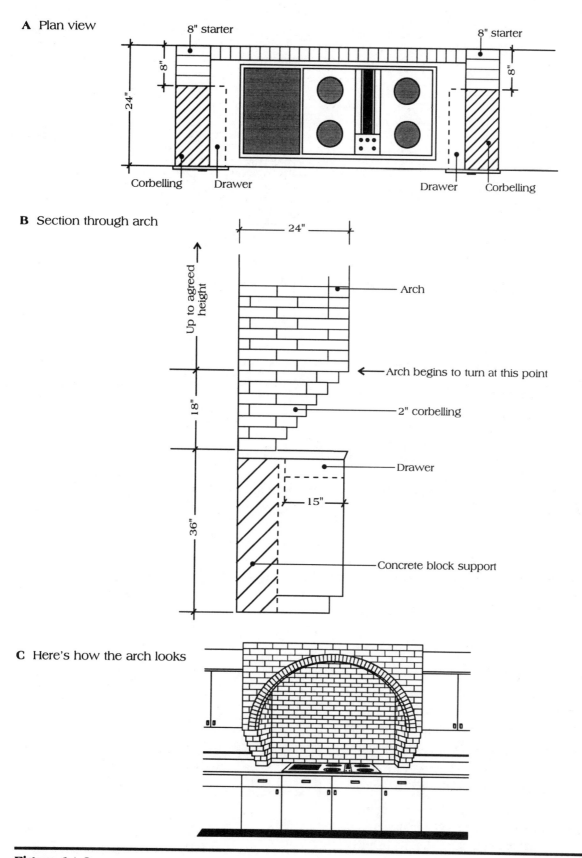

A Plan view

8" starter

8"

24"

Corbelling   Drawer   8" starter

8"

Drawer   Corbelling

B Section through arch

24"

Up to agreed height

Arch

Arch begins to turn at this point

2" corbelling

18"

Drawer

15"

36"

Concrete block support

C Here's how the arch looks

Figure 14-9
Use corbels to support the arch and gain counter space

A This arrangement wastes space

B This recessed arrangement is better

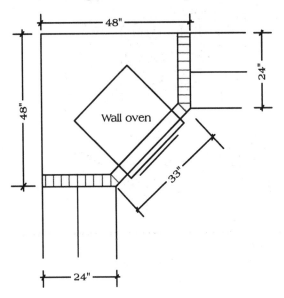

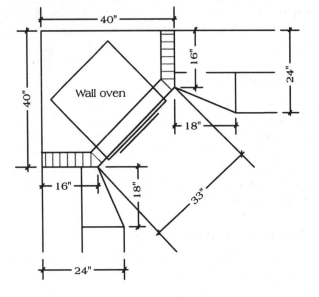

Figure 14-10
A wall oven installed in a corner

now being used in kitchens just for decoration. Don't be afraid to suggest the unusual to your clients. Here are some unusual treatments that can help create a truly unique kitchen.

Glass, Plain or Stained

Stained glass creates a customized accent at modest cost. Glass on cabinet doors, especially those over a peninsula, relieves the massive look of solid doors. Besides its obvious use in windows, you can also use stained glass panels in exterior doors or side lights, and for interior French or bi-fold doors.

Figure 14-11 A shows a stained glass design based on European windows made many centuries ago. In the center of the circle is the family crest, logo or monogram. Figure 14-11 B shows what's usually called bottle glass. These discs aren't really bottle ends. But the origin of the name is obvious.

Don't overlook mirrors as a wallcovering material for kitchens. They add brightness and make a room seem larger. You never have to paint them, and they're easy to clean with a swipe of glass cleaner and a paper towel.

Decorative Grille Wire

Wire overlays, such as those shown in Figure 14-12, can be used effectively for cabinets anywhere you want a change in texture. These grilles come in brass, antiqued copper or bronze, and satin-finish stainless steel. They're generally installed over glass panels which can be removed from inside the cabinet for easy cleaning.

A Stained glass   **B** Bottle glass

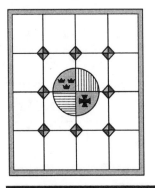

Figure 14-11
Decorative glass

Plastics

The vertical rods in Figure 14-13 are clear Lucite. You can get these in a wide range of diameters and lengths. Used this way in a peninsula, they suggest a divider between rooms without creating a solid visual barrier.

Exposed Beams

These can be structural, or merely decorative "plant-ons." They add authenticity to rustic or antique decorating styles. But don't get carried away. Too many can be overpowering. Exposed beams aren't necessarily solid. You can build them from ¾-inch boards, which, like their solid counterparts, can be rough-sawn, distressed, or smooth.

Other Decorative Finishes

Use paneling that matches the cabinets to add a cozy warmth to a large kitchen, but be sure there's enough light to compensate for the darker walls. Wallpaper is also effective to add interest. Use it on soffits or in the areas between upper and lower cabinets. Many wallpapers suitable for kitchens have matching fabrics available for use in upholstery or window coverings.

If your customer is a gourmet or a collector of antique kitchenware, provide attractive ways to display decorative or bulky utensils where they're easy to see and reach. Use copper, brass, iron, chrome or wooden hangers that match the style of your kitchen design.

Because today's kitchen is the family's gathering place for many activities besides preparing, eating, and cleaning up after meals, the kitchen must be comfortable and attractive as well as functional. Take advantage of the wide range of kitchen materials available, and your kitchen designs will look as good as they work.

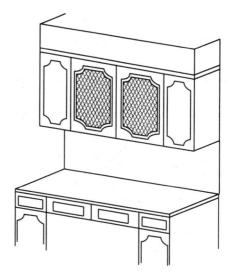

Figure 14-12
Grille wire overlay on cabinet door

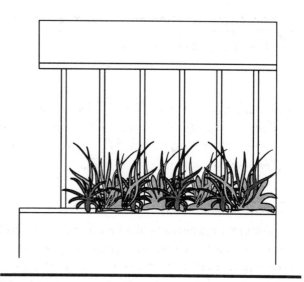

Figure 14-13
Lucite rods create an "invisible" barrier

Test Questions for Chapter 14

1. Before you install brick veneer in a kitchen with a conventional floor over a basement or crawl space, how can you make sure that it will safely support the additional weight?

2. You can use a plywood panel to distribute the weight of any brickwork you are going to install. How should you cut it before you attach it to the floor?

3. What advantages does cored brick have over solid brick?

4. What is the standard formula for mortar used for laying brick?

5. Since brick are porous and easily stained by spattering grease, it's a good idea to have them sealed against moisture. What would you use to seal the brick?

6. What do you install after every fifth course in a freestanding brick wall to make it more stable?

7. Name two advantages of building a cavity wall instead of a solid brick wall.

8. How would you secure a 4-inch brick wall to an existing wall?

9. What are the advantages of facing a wall with split brick instead of whole brick?

10. What was accomplished by corbeling the brick arch in Figure 14-9?

CHAPTER 15
Your Kitchen Design Business

Starting any business takes confidence in your own ability. It also takes patience and money. Without those, no amount of talent and exposure will assure your success.

Only you know if you have the confidence to run your own business. If you're confident, do you have the patience? Not many businesses flourish immediately. It takes time to learn the ropes and build the customer base you need to keep busy. You have to be willing to let your business grow at a reasonable pace. Don't try to bite off more than you can chew at the beginning.

And what about the money? It can be a little or a lot – but of course, the more the better. As a rule of thumb, assume you'll need at least six months of living expenses set aside as a cushion while you're getting started. Many people have launched successful businesses with much less, but it's not easy. Lack of capital is the leading cause of new business failures. Plan carefully. The extra work and long hours should pay off in the long run, if you're good at what you do.

Consider starting your kitchen design business as a sideline while you stay at your present job. Another way to work your way into the kitchen design business is to work as a salesperson for a large appliance retailer. Or, you may be able to rent space from an appliance or cabinet dealer and sell your design services that way. At the same time, you'll be collecting sales commissions. In either case, you'll build your reputation and gain experience, but without all the risks and expense of going out entirely on your own.

Startup Costs

No matter how small you start out, it still costs money. Even if you work from home and don't have to pay rent for an office or store, there are a few things you can't do without.

First, you need to get a separate phone line for your business. It's unprofessional and often a nuisance to use your home phone, especially if your family includes kids. Then, you need to buy an ad in the yellow pages of your local phone directory – even if you don't advertise anywhere else at first.

You'll need stationery and business cards, and perhaps signs for your vehicle. It's also a good idea to have signs you can post on jobs where you're working (with your client's consent, of course).

Most communities require a business license. In some states you'll have to post a sales tax deposit with the taxing agency if you have to charge sales tax.

Name Your Business

Before you apply for a business license or phone number, decide on a name for your company. Of course, you can use your own name, but it's often better to pick a name that people will remember and readily associate with your services. Look through the yellow pages for the names of your competitors. Avoid picking a name that's confusingly similar to names other companies are using. If possible, pick a name that starts at the beginning of the alphabet. That puts you near the top of your classification in the phone book, where most shoppers start looking.

If you use a name other than your own, you'll probably have to file a Fictitious Business Name Statement, or DBA (doing business as). Your local newspaper can usually help with that. They'll file your form with the proper agency, and run the required ad in their Legal Notices section.

Set Up Your Workplace

Select a place where you can work uninterrupted, a comfortable place where you can sit down with your clients to discuss their needs. It can be a rented space, or even a room in your own home. You don't need an expensive office with a receptionist or an elaborate showroom. If you have confidence in your ability, a humble beginning shouldn't present any obstacle.

Your office should have a table or drawing board, a place for plans, a file cabinet, a desk, and at least two chairs besides your own. If you have diplomas or certificates which attest to your expertise, frame them attractively and hang them where your customers will see them.

Get Access to a Showroom

Most medium-to-large cities have manufacturers' design showrooms. These are often open to the trade only, not the general public. But you can take clients to these showrooms. There they'll see the latest in cabinets, appliances and accessories. Find the showrooms in your area and register with them.

Know Your Products

By now you know there's much more to kitchen design than sticking some cabinets and appliances into a room. To be worthy of your client's trust, you have to know everything about the latest in appliances and fixtures. Be able to describe special features in detail. And while no one can be expected to memorize hundreds of costs, keep your catalogs and price lists well organized so you have the latest information at your fingertips. Few things make you look less professional than having to plow through messy piles of paper to find the information your customer wants.

Finding Customers

You might be the best kitchen designer in the world, but you'll never make a dime if you don't have any customers. Let's talk about some ways to get them.

Advertise

We've already mentioned the phone book, probably your most cost-effective place to advertise a service business. Once you start to make money so your advertising budget increases (if you base your budget on a percentage of gross sales), you can begin looking for other good places to run ads.

Local newspapers can be a good bet. Their display ads cost less than the big-city newspapers, and they target customers in your neighborhood. Some papers publish a special home-improvement tabloid several times a year which will put your ad in front of the people who are most likely to need your services.

Print a clever flyer and pay your kids (or your neighbors' kids) to pass them out. Don't, however, put flyers under windshield wipers in shopping centers. People resent littering today, and most of those flyers wind up all over the parking lot or along the roadside.

Contact General Contractors

Many contractors are too busy with their own specialty, or the day-to-day problems of running their businesses, to concentrate much on the details of kitchen design. But they also realize that a well-planned kitchen is a major point of appeal for new home buyers. Spec builders in particular may be willing to work with you. Keep a mailing list of contractors in your area. Send a letter to them every few months, reminding them of your services. Enclose a business card, or even an inexpensive promotional item of some kind. Eventually they may need your help, and your name will come to mind.

Contact Former Clients

Building a business is a long and sometimes discouraging process. But there are things you can do to improve the odds of success. If you've worked in an architect's office or appliance showroom before going out on your own, contact the people who have seen your work there. Stress your ability, of which they already have evidence, and your willingness to work closely with them on any future work they may be planning. I don't feel that this is unethical. Their relationship to your former employer ended when the project was finished. They're now free to select anyone they want to work with. Your business card is the best possible advertising. Send it to people you've worked with, announcing that you're available for kitchen design business. Ask them for referrals to family and friends.

Get Lists of New Projects

Visit your local building department or planning office occasionally. Find out who has drawn residential permits. Some are building their own homes. Other will be spec builders. Both may find your service useful.

Socialize

Don't meet anyone without letting them know what you do. Join your local Chamber of Commerce or a service club and attend their meetings and social activities. Keep your business cards handy. Spread the word around where you bowl or play golf. Word-of-mouth and personal recommendations are the best (and cheapest) form of advertising.

If your ad budget permits, sponsor a bowling or little league team, or buy ads in programs for local school activities. While these aren't the most productive kinds of advertising, in a small community they do reinforce your name recognition and reputation for community involvement.

Talk, Talk, Talk

I've been on radio talk shows several times, offering advice to listeners who need home-improvement advice. Write to the radio station, in care of the program director or producers. Addresses will be in your local phone book. If you enjoy talking to groups, be available as a guest speaker at decorating seminars or trade meetings.

Offer to put on a course on kitchen design at your local community college. The income won't be very much, but the students will be people who may need your service.

Follow Up with Good Customer Relations

Once you've got the customers, take good care of them. Make sure you, your employees and your subcontractors are courteous and reliable. If you or someone who works for you will be late for an appointment, be sure the customer is notified. Nothing builds sales resistance quicker than a salesman late for an appointment.

If you make a mistake on a job, be quick and thorough about fixing the problem. Build a reputation for reliability. People talk about their kitchen jobs the same way they talk about their doctor or lawyer. Do good work and the word will get around.

A Showroom of Your Own

When you can afford it, set up a showroom-office in a busy shopping center or on a high-traffic thoroughfare with easy access and good parking. Make the signs on your building eye-catching and attractive.

The inside of your storefront office must be neat, clean, well-lighted and easy to move around in. Arrange samples attractively and within easy reach. People love to touch things, and they're intimidated if things are locked away in cases or displayed where they can't be seen up close.

Arrange a comfortable spot for customers to sit during your consultation, or while they're looking through catalogs and brochures. If you have photos of kitchens you've designed, display them attractively in this area, so you can use them to illustrate features you recommend for the customer's new kitchen. Separate this area from the display part of the showroom, where other customers will be a distraction.

Many suppliers provide samples of their products at no charge. Set aside separate sections for such things as countertop materials and flooring. A small showroom won't have space for more than a few hardware samples. But try to display at least a few of the most popular styles and colors.

Use Space Wisely

As a kitchen designer, your sales will suffer if you're not also a good showroom designer. If your showroom is small, the biggest challenge is making it comprehensive, yet attractive.

Be practical, but show off your flair for design. Leave room for people to move around. You don't want your showroom to feel like a crowded, cluttered supermarket. In places where aisles are narrow, people looking for something on one side are blocked by those looking on the other, or by shoppers passing in front of them. Also, it's hard to see what you're looking for when you have to look at a display from top to bottom at close range.

This same principle applies to a showroom. Space your displays so that there's room for people to walk around them comfortably without interference. If you display appliances, there should be enough room to fully open a refrigerator door, or pull out a dishwasher rack to show its special features.

Arrange Displays for Best Effect

Avoid arranging your showroom in "columns and rows." Set some of your displays diagonally. Arrange others back-to-back with a divider or partition between them. Use island displays that customers can walk all the way around.

Try to allow room for at least one complete kitchen vignette, even if it's a tiny one. People get distracted if all they see are components. It's comforting to see a whole kitchen, even if it's not exactly what the customer has in mind.

Display at least one economy line of cabinets. Make that display as attractive as possible. Show at least two of the more expensive lines as well. Select models which are very different from one another in appearance, but include components which show off all the best features. Place the different grades close together so your client will see the advantages of the more expensive selections. You'll find it easier to sell up when comparisons are easier.

And never put two displays with the same shade of wood or color next to each other. Sameness detracts from interest. Contrast is the word to remember when arranging displays.

Lighting Is Important

Lighting is as important in a showroom as it is in a kitchen. A bright showroom invites approach. It also shows the displays better than if the light is subdued. Use several spots or swivel hi-hats directed at certain features you wish to give prominence. That serves two purposes. It emphasizes your display, and it helps you sell light fixtures. And be sure to include some under-cabinet lighting.

Pay Attention to the Colors

As a rule, bright colors attract. But try to combine them so they don't clash. No part of the display will get the attention it deserves if that happens.

Contrast is necessary, but the amount of color is more important. I proved this when I had to introduce a new product in a card in a New York subway car. To make the message noticed, I made part of it in large, bold letters in a subdued tone, while the heart of the message was in much smaller letters, but in an eye-catching bright color. Because of the proportions, neither element took too much attention from the other. That's the secret: Contrast in moderation.

The same approach can be used effectively when displaying a section of cabinets. If one is of a dark-toned wood, try to place it near a lighter section. Never let the countertop material take attention away from the cabinets: it plays a secondary role. If the cabinets are light, use a darker color countertop as contrast. They will complement each other.

Hiring Help

As your business grows, you'll probably need additional salespeople, and very likely some office help. When time is precious, delegate routine jobs to others. Concentrate on supervising your staff, serving customers and managing your company.

Look for Personality

When hiring salespeople, look for personality and expertise. The first of these, personality, takes some intuition on your part. Avoid people with too forceful a personality. "High-power" salespeople can produce sales. But they're more likely to antagonize the type of client you need most.

How do I know this? When my kitchen business was growing, I started getting more calls than I could handle. In short, I needed another salesman. Of the applicants, I chose the one that impressed me the most. He was bright, knowledgeable about kitchens, smooth-spoken and quite likable. He charmed the customers, and they believed everything he said he could do for them. He sounds great, doesn't he?

But it wasn't long before complaints started coming in. It seems he was promising more than he was writing into the contracts, and his customers wanted to know why his promises weren't kept. That didn't leave me much choice. To save my credibility and reputation, I had to do most of what he had promised – even though it wasn't in the contract or in the estimate. I fired him just in time. If I'd had to cover many more of those "freebies," I would have been out of business.

Luckily, my business survived, and I learned a lesson. Look out for those glib-talking salespeople. Always check what they put in the contracts, and make sure the customers know what they're entitled to get. That keeps problems at a minimum, and your reputation intact.

Expertise Is Just as Important

Finding expertise is harder. Basically, how good is this person at designing kitchens? To find out, first ask how long they've been designing kitchens. Has it been for a firm that handles cut-rate cabinets, or more expensive, custom-made units? This is important to know if you're aiming at a more affluent customer base.

When you're bidding a job against a competitor, your company's superb design can eliminate the opposition, even if your price is higher. Ask how long the candidate has been in the business. Why does he or she want to work for you? And why did they leave their last job?

Before you hire anyone, for sales or any other position, call their former employer. Ask about their reliability, and what their best and worst traits are. Find out whether the former employer would rehire this individual. If not, why not?

Finally, you may want to devise a test for the most promising candidates. Use a standard kitchen plan, and ask how they could improve on it. If you do kitchen remodels, also ask them what the construction would involve. Do they know enough about plumbing, wiring and framing to understand what's feasible and what's not? An attractive and innovative design is worthless if it can't be accomplished within the home-owner's budget.

Keep Your Credit Record Clean

At the beginning of this chapter, I cautioned you to start out slowly and not bite off more than you can chew. I emphasize that here, because that's probably the second reason why most new businesses fail.

Shop wisely when you buy materials, services and supplies for your business. Take the time to get competitive bids whenever they're available. When you're dealing with a sole source, try to negotiate better prices based on volume or credit history. Pay your bills on time, take advantage of discounts based on prompt payment, and maintain good financial records. When you're ready to hit the big time, your good credit record, and the working capital accumulated in your business, will make your banker much more accommodating in providing the financing you need to grow.

Test Questions for Chapter 15

1. What must you have, above all else, to start your own business?

2. What is the rule of thumb for how much capital you should have to start your business?

3. Even if you start your business from your home, what is the one thing which you must have?

4. When naming your business, what should you look for?

5. Clients will want to be able to see model kitchens and appliances. How can you provide that service?

6. What's the first step you should take to find customers?

7. Why is it a good idea to send a letter to general contractors every few months?

8. What are some of the essentials in a showroom that attract clients?

9. What are the two main things you should look for when you need to hire a salesperson?

10. In hiring, how might you determine an applicant's design expertise?

Answers for Chapter 1

1. The prime objective in kitchen design is to make the kitchen functional and convenient. *(Page 6)*

2. The five Basic Rules for counter placement are: put counters at both sides of the sink, on both sides of the cooktop, on at least one side of a wall oven, on the opening side of the refrigerator and on the opening side of the pantry door. *(Page 6)*

3. Allow at least 24 to 36 inches of counter space between the sink and a cooktop or oven. *(Page 6)*

4. A cooktop at the end of a counter would permit pot handles to protrude beyond the counter end. This can be very dangerous. *(Page 8)*

5. It allows storage of regularly-used items right where they're needed. No one likes to have to go into the garage or the basement every time they need something. *(Page 10)*

6. You can install lazy Susans and carousels to provide more usable space in corner cabinets. *(Page 15)*

7. No two people use the kitchen the same way, or have the same needs and preferences. Make your kitchen design fit the needs of the homeowners. *(Page 18)*

8. The architect's scale is divided into inches, while the engineer's scale is divided into decimals, or tenths of a foot. Kitchen cabinets and appliances are dimensioned in feet and inches, not in decimals of a foot. *(Pages 19-20)*

9. If you have a room layout prepared in advance, you'll know, when you make your plans, what units and appliances will fit. There's no point creating a brilliant plan on paper if it's not going to fit in the kitchen you're planning it for. *(Page 20)*

10. When you use standard symbols properly, it gives your plans a professional look, and helps anyone using them to understand exactly what you want. *(Pages 20 and 24)*

Answers for Chapter 2

1. Although a one-wall kitchen has limited space, it must still contain all the necessary appliances and storage. That means you must make every inch count. *(Page 27)*

2. In a one-wall kitchen, it's best to place the range and refrigerator at opposite ends of the wall, with the sink in between. *(Page 27)*

3. If you install small fluorescent lights under the upper cabinets, they'll provide light directly on the countertops, eliminating the problem of shadows from ceiling lighting. *(Page 27)*

4. To maximize storage space in a small kitchen, make the upper cabinet shelves adjustable. You can also install roll-out shelves in the base cabinets so all their contents are fully accessible. *(Pages 28-29)*

5. To add more storage space without changing the kitchen layout, you can install a full-length cabinet over the sink, which adds an additional shelf. You can also add narrow shelves under the wall cabinets for small items. *(Pages 29-30)*

6. To make the space under the sink more useful, install a roll-out shelf in the sink base cabinet. It can hold many small items without interfering with the plumbing or garbage disposal. *(Page 29)*

7. In a corridor kitchen, the distance between cabinet fronts on facing walls should never be less than 36 inches. If it's less than this, whenever one of the appliances is open, the passageway will be blocked. *(Page 30)*

8. Avoid placing the wall oven and dishwasher opposite each other. When both are in use, the open doors completely block the passageway. *(Pages 30-31)*

9. The stove should be on the same wall as the sink in a corridor kitchen to avoid the possibility of a collision between someone carrying a hot pot from the range to the sink, and someone passing through the kitchen. *(Page 32)*

10. You should always provide separate end support for a countertop, even when there will be a dishwasher there to support it, because someone may put weight on the countertop before the dishwasher is installed, or if it is removed for repair or replacement. Without support, it could break. *(Page 34)*

Answers for Chapter 3

1. One way to visually unify a kitchen is to add a valance between sections of cabinets. This makes them appear to be one continuous unit. And the valance hides the light fixture over the sink. *(Page 38)*

2. It is important that soffits conform to the shape of the upper cabinets in a kitchen, or they will form spaces that collect dust. *(Page 39)*

3. The benefit of indenting the sink cabinet is that you gain more room to use the dishwasher. And it's easier to reach the cabinet over the sink. *(Page 39)*

4. To make the space under a wall oven more usable, replace the shelves with a drawer that slides out. This makes the whole space accessible. *(Page 41)*

5. Leaving an 11-inch wall space between the edge of the wall oven and the doorway permits easier entrance to the kitchen. *(Page 42)*

6. Moving the refrigerator to its position in Figure 3-12 allows both the freezer and the refrigerator doors to open fully, and puts the countertop on the correct side for convenient use. *(Page 42)*

7. Moving the refrigerator 20 inches in from the doorway allows enough space for the doorway. It also provides space for a shallow pantry. *(Pages 42-43)*

8. This kitchen has several good design elements. Both the refrigerator and cooktop have adequate counter space. The corner sink creates an efficient work triangle, and there's plenty of storage space. *(Page 44)*

9. To add a pantry without reducing the counter space, you can use an undercounter pantry. *(Page 44)*

10. Installing a window lets in natural light and makes the kitchen appear more spacious. By using a small one, you still have room for a 16-inch-high cabinet above it. *(Page 45)*

Answers for Chapter 4

1. A U-shaped kitchen is the easiest to design because it has three walls to work with, making it easy to locate the major appliances according to the five Basic Rules. *(Page 47)*

2. The kitchen in Figure 4-1 has several design flaws. One wall is completely bare and wasted, there are dead corners both in the uppers and bases, and there's very little counter space. *(Pages 47-48)*

3. The most obvious design flaw in Figure 4-3 is the location of the refrigerator. It's at the far end of the room, much too far from the sink, and creating a work triangle far longer than is acceptable. *(Page 49)*

4. Redesigning the kitchen put the refrigerator closer, provided counter space beside both the refrigerator and the wall oven, and significantly increased the usable cabinet space. *(Pages 50-52)*

5. Removing the non-bearing wall opened up the use of the kitchen. Now, people sitting at the table can see and converse with those in the kitchen. It also provides a pass-through between the kitchen and the dining area, saving many steps. *(Pages 52-53)*

6. Installing a kitty-corner sink, because it's set back into what was largely unreachable counter space, frees up accessible counter space. Indenting it leaves room to stand at the side of the open dishwasher to load or unload it. *(Page 52)*

7. Placing the base cabinet between the sink and the refrigerator provided storage for silverware next to the sink, and the all-important countertop space next to the refrigerator. *(Page 52)*

8. Reversing the swing of the doors means that they don't interfere with the new pantry door. *(Page 53)*

9. Some of the benefits gained in redesigning the kitchen in Figure 4-8 are: When the short end wall near the refrigerator was removed, it allowed the refrigerator door to open completely. A dead corner was made useful. And an extra wall cabinet was gained on each side of the window. *(Page 53)*

10. Installing a continuous soffit would improve the appearance of the kitchen, by unifying the upper cabinets, but it would not improve the utility of the kitchen. Generally, a good kitchen designer will not leave a wall empty. The space should be used for storage, which is always at a premium in a kitchen. *(Page 53)*

Answers for Chapter 5

1. A peninsula kitchen gives greater access to the adjoining room and helps alleviate the closed-in feeling one can get in a small kitchen. It also provides more countertop space and more cabinets. *(Page 57)*

2. It's especially important to consider the height of your client when you're designing a peninsula kitchen because if you place uppers over a peninsula, they can block the view of a tall person. But if you set them high to avoid this, a short person may not be able to reach them. *(Pages 57-58)*

3. Cabinets over a peninsula are usually set with a distance of 24 inches between the countertop and the bottom of the uppers. *(Page 58)*

4. To vent a cooking appliance on a peninsula, you can either install a range with a venting system which draws fumes down into a vent line leading to the outside, or you can use a vented hood attached to the underside of the cabinet over the range. *(Page 59)*

5. Fans are measured in the number of cubic feet of air the fan can move per minute (CFM). The higher the CFM on an exhaust fan, the greater the exhausting power. *(Page 59)*

6. The upper cabinet on a peninsula must be set back at least 3 inches from the end of the peninsula to prevent head injury when a person steps close to the base cabinet. *(Page 60)*

7. To run the 2-inch drain from the sink on a peninsula, you can either go through the toe space under the cabinets, or, if there's a crawl space, under the floor. *(Page 61)*

8. When you're installing a built-in blender or food-processor base, it's best to choose a flat surface like wood, plastic laminate or marble for the countertop. Avoid tile, if possible. *(Page 62)*

9. Using clear or stained-glass doors on upper peninsula cabinets allows light through and eliminates the closed-in feeling that solid cabinets might cause. It's also a nice decorative effect. *(Page 62)*

10. To design a functional peninsula in a kitchen, the kitchen needs to be at least 7 feet wide. That provides 36 inches between the facing base cabinets. It's better to leave 48 inches if possible. *(Page 64)*

Answers for Chapter 6

1. A kitchen must have at least 8 feet of open space for an island to be installed. *(Page 69)*

2. An island must be surrounded on all sides by at least 36 inches of open space, but 42 inches is better. *(Page 69)*

3. You shouldn't place any appliance at the end of an island, or a peninsula. There always needs to be counter space on both sides. *(Page 69)*

4. The correct counter height for an island, if the seating is stools, is 36 inches. If the seating is chairs, the counter height should be 28 to 30 inches. *(Page 69)*

5. There are several major design flaws in the kitchen shown in Figure 6-2: The wall oven has no countertop adjacent to it. The cooktop is at right angles to the sink – always an inconvenient layout. And in general, there's a lot of wasted space in this large kitchen.
(Pages 70-71)

6. To improve the refrigerator wall shown in Figure 6-4 C, you could extend the soffit over the cabinets flanking the refrigerator. That would prevent that "in and out" look. You could also put lights behind the soffits to light the countertops below. *(Page 72)*

7. Design flaws in the kitchen in Figure 6-6 are: The cooktop has a dead corner on both sides. The location of the refrigerator means that the cook can't stand in front of the open oven door. The narrow space in front of the refrigerator is the only entrance to the kitchen, and it's blocked when the refrigerator door is open. *(Page 72)*

8. The dishwasher location in Figure 6-10 A is unworkable because it is not near the sink, where dishes can be scraped into the disposal then loaded directly. Nor is it near the cabinets where the dishes are stored. *(Page 75)*

9. A peninsula with no cabinets above, even if the intent is to leave an unobstructed view into the other room, is still a waste of space. You can have both upper cabinets and an unobstructed view by simply installing uppers with 24 inches of clear space between them and the countertop. *(Page 75)*

10. In the kitchen in Figure 6-12, moving the dishwasher to the right of the sink made room for a silverware drawer next to the sink. Putting in a 5-inch filler strip made more room to work at the sink when the dishwasher is open. *(Page 78)*

Answers for Chapter 7

1. The biggest design flaw in the kitchen in Figure 7-1 is that you have to detour around the peninsula to get from the kitchen to the breakfast area, or from there to the dining room. The owner found this confining and inconvenient. *(Page 81)*

2. Other obvious errors are that when the wall oven door is open, it restricts access to the dining room. Also, the snack bar is too close to the cooktop. And the counter space is on the wrong side of the refrigerator. *(Pages 81-82)*

3. Curving the sink wall cabinets provided space for a pantry and wine cabinet at the ends. *(Pages 81-82)*

4. To meet fire safety regulations when making the new closet behind the refrigerator open into the garage, you can line the wall with 2 inches of masonry and ½ inch of drywall. *(Pages 81-82)*

5. The eating counter was made deep to move the occupants farther from the cooktop. It also made it easier for them to see and talk to each other. *(Page 82)*

6. A rolling cart would be impractical if the flooring is uneven tile or flagstone. You shouldn't make a rolling cart unless the flooring is smooth. *(Page 82)*

7. If the existing floor can't support the weight of the masonry you're proposing to put around a wall oven, you would have to reinforce the floor joists to safely support the extra load. Remember to include that extra work in your bid. *(Page 84)*

8. In Figure 7-3, the archway holding the grill is set at an angle to increase the visibility of the decorative brickwork, to provide easy venting to an outside wall, and to allow more counter space around the grill. *(Page 84)*

9. To make the island in Figure 7-3 more useful, we installed a food processor base. We also made the overhang extra deep, so the user can sit comfortably while working at the island. *(Page 85)*

10. A light fixture over an island allows you to add pan-display beams to the fixture, as shown in Figure 7-3. Shiny copper or brass utensils hanging from these beams provide an appealing centerpiece for the kitchen. *(Page 85)*

Answers for Chapter 8

1. Most raw lumber is seasoned by being placed on racks to dry in the air. Better-quality lumber is kiln-dried to a standard 8 percent moisture content. *(Page 87)*

2. Two types of laminated cabinet material used today are plycore, which usually has a 5-layer core faced with veneer, and lumber core, which has a single ply of veneer over a solid core. *(Page 87)*

3. Careful measuring is important on any construction work, but while a mistake by a framer may waste a piece of lumber, if you measure a kitchen wrong and order cabinets and countertops that won't fit, it's going to cost you a lot more than a piece of lumber. *(Page 88)*

4. A good rule to keep in mind when measuring for cabinets and countertops is that the walls are never exactly flush, vertical or parallel, that corners are rarely 90 degrees, and that the floor and ceiling are seldom parallel. *(Page 88)*

5. It's necessary to remove the toe space base before tilting a floor-to-ceiling cabinet into place because the diagonal height of the cabinet is greater than the floor-to-ceiling height. It will hit the ceiling before it stands upright. *(Page 89)*

6. The disadvantage of having a stile separate two doors of a cabinet is that it makes it more difficult to remove objects from the cabinet. *(Page 92)*

7. The major difference between less expensive and more expensive drawers is in the joints. More expensive cabinetry has dovetailed joints. Less expensive drawers usually have stapled frames with Masonite bottoms that fit in a groove. *(Page 92)*

8. When installing an undercounter pantry that's only 12 inches deep, it's best if it opens from the wider side. If it opened from the 12-inch side, there wouldn't be enough usable space on the shelves. *(Page 96)*

9. When the base corner cabinet is angled, the upper cabinet above it should also be angled. If you use standard corner cabinets, it will be too hard to reach into them. *(Pages 97-98)*

10. Upper cabinets should always be installed first. If you install the lowers first, you're going to have to climb over them to get to the wall to install the uppers. This is not only a major inconvenience, but there's a good chance the lowers will be damaged in the process. *(Page 98)*

Answers for Chapter 9

1. When choosing a sink where counter space is limited, it's best to use a 24-inch single-bowl sink. It saves counter and cabinet space, but is still large enough to wash large pans. *(Page 103)*

2. A more-practical variation of the standard two-bowl sink has one large bowl and one small one, instead of two equal-sized bowls. The large bowl will hold large pans, while the small one is good for rinsing food or dishes. *(Page 104)*

3. A disadvantage of three-bowl sinks are that they require a large base cabinet. Since you always need counter space on both sides of a sink, these can only be used in larger kitchens. Another disadvantage is that none of the bowls is big enough to hold large pans. *(Page 104)*

4. When installing a corner sink with a dishwasher next to it, you should place a 5-inch filler between the dishwasher and sink. This allows room to stand at the sink when the dishwasher door is open. *(Page 105)*

5. Places where you might install secondary sinks are in peninsulas, in islands, or in wet bars. *(Page 105)*

6. The worst disadvantage of stainless steel sinks is that they show every water spot, requiring constant wiping to look good. Other problems are that the surface is easily scratched, that some household chemicals can discolor them, and that they're noisier than enameled cast iron sinks. *(Page 106)*

7. Sinks installed below countertop level and integral molded sinks make it easier to keep the countertop clean. This is because they don't have a raised edge to keep you from sweeping spills straight into the sink. *(Page 106)*

8. When you install a sink in an island or peninsula on a slab floor, you'll have to cut a channel in the slab to make room for the plumbing lines. *(Page 106)*

9. To keep sewer gas from entering the house, you should install a P-trap. The water in the trap forms a seal. *(Pages 106-107)*

10. Local water conservation requirements may mandate flow restrictors, and you may not be allowed to install certain types of water softeners or purification systems. *(Page 107)*

Answers for Chapter 10

1. The standard sizes for freestanding ranges are 30 or 36 inches wide, although a 24-inch width is also available. *(Page 109)*

2. Since electric cooktops are much shallower than gas ones, you can usually install a drawer under the cooktop to hold utensils. *(Page 110)*

3. When a cooktop is set into an island or a peninsula, you can vent it without installing an exhaust hood above by installing a down-draft unit. This can be vented up through a wall or along the floor beams to the outside. *(Page 111)*

4. A kitchen exhaust system should be able to circulate the room air about 15 times per hour. *(Page 112)*

5. The minimum fan capacity for a wall-mounted exhaust fan is at least 100 CFM per linear foot of hood length. *(Page 112)*

6. The fan capacity for an exhaust fan over an island or peninsula should be at least 120 CFM per linear foot. *(Page 112)*

7. The distance from the counter to the bottom of a wall-mounted exhaust hood should be at least 20 inches, although 24 inches is better for taller cooks. *(Pages 112-113)*

8. It's a good idea, when you install a freestanding refrigerator between two base cabinets, to eliminate the small spaces created between the refrigerator and the cabinets. These spaces are a constant nuisance, collecting unreachable spills and dropped objects. To do it, enclose the refrigerator with the same material as the cabinets. *(Page 116)*

9. You shouldn't place a dishwasher at right angles to the sink because the open dishwasher door will block access to the sink. *(Page 118)*

10. The advantages of trash bins over trash compactors are that they don't use energy, they're trouble-free, they're much cheaper, and the face of the bin can be made to match the cabinets. *(Page 118)*

Answers for Chapter 11

1. Installing built-in small appliances keeps them readily available, while not taking up valuable space on the countertop. *(Page 121)*

2. When installing a built-in can opener over a countertop, be sure to place it high enough that tall cans, such as coffee or shortening cans, will fit in the space. *(Page 121)*

3. A good plan when installing a food center flush in a countertop is to build a narrow drawer in the space next to it. This drawer should have a full-size front so it matches the rest of the cabinets, and can be used for storing the machine's accessories. See Figure 11-2. *(Page 122)*

4. For heavy appliances like mixers, there's a lift-up shelf made specifically for this. It swings up and locks in place, providing its own counter space. It's easily installed in a standard base cabinet. *(Page 123)*

5. One way of storing spices is to construct a shallow (about 7 inches deep) built-in cabinet that has door shelves as well as inner shelves. This can be mounted in a spot that's too small for a regular-size cabinet. Another way to store spices is to outfit a drawer with dividers that hold spice bottles at an angle, where they are easy to see and reach. *(Page 123)*

6. To provide space for soda cans and bottles, you can install a convenient, slide-out unit that takes about 12 to 15 inches in a base cabinet. It needs strong tracks to carry the weight. *(Page 124)*

7. For storage of grains and baking needs, you can mount a handy little unit with several scoop-shaped compartments on the wall or under an upper cabinet. *(Page 124)*

8. The space under an electric cooktop is perfect for a shallow drawer with partitions to hold knives, spatulas, and other flat utensils needed for cooking. *(Page 124)*

9. An ideal way to use dead space at the end of a peninsula is to build in slide-out racks for hanging tablecloths. This puts them right where they are needed, and doesn't take up valuable drawer space. *(Page 124-125)*

10. When you install a garden window, make sure it's in a location where children won't be playing, or else high enough that projecting corners aren't a danger. *(Page 125)*

Answers for Chapter 12

1. The primary purpose of underlayment is to create a smooth, even surface. It also provides solid support for the finish flooring. *(Page 127)*

2. Materials used for underlayment are oriented strand board (OSB) or flakeboard, plywood, and hardboard (Masonite). Each, if properly installed, should create a good underlayment. *(Page 128)*

3. After laying the underlayment, and before laying a brick floor, you must fasten waterproofed tarpaper to the underlayment, or to the existing floor. Follow that with a layer of portland cement with 16 gauge wire mesh embedded. *(Page 128)*

4. Although carpeting is comfortable, it soils and stains easily. With the constant spills that occur in a kitchen, carpeting is going to look shabby in no time. It can also get torn or scuffed when heavy appliances are moved over it. *(Page 128)*

5. The main drawbacks of ceramic tile as flooring are that it's not very comfortable to walk or stand on for long periods of time, it's cold, slippery when wet, and it costs more, both to buy and to install, than most other types of flooring. *(Page 128)*

6. To save on the amount of tile you need on a kitchen floor, you can use plywood or concrete board instead of tile under major appliances. *(Page 129)*

7. When removing old resilient tile or sheet flooring, which may contain asbestos, try not to create any dust, and wear a mask or respirator. *(Page 129)*

8. The tools for removing resilient sheet flooring would be a scraper, a utility or hook knife, and a high-efficiency vacuum cleaner. *(Page 129)*

9. You can level an uneven concrete subfloor with a latex preparation designed for that purpose. You'll find it at a masonry supply dealer. *(Page 130)*

10. Diagonal installation of wood flooring provides greater structural strength, since it always spans the subfloor joists. It can also save you from having to change direction in an L- or T-shaped room. *(Page 131)*

Answers for Chapter 13

1. A fixture with three 60-watt bulbs will provide the 175 to 200 watts of lighting required for each 50 square feet of floor space. *(Page 133)*

2. A foot-candle is the amount of light thrown by a candle onto a square foot surface 1 foot away from the candle. *(Page 133)*

3. For daytime lighting, install skylights or "sun tubes" where possible. *(Page 134)*

4. Use indirect lighting for kitchens with high or cathedral ceilings. It illuminates the wall or ceiling as well as the space below. *(Page 134)*

5. To install dome lighting, you need at least 12 inches above the upper cabinets. *(Page 135)*

6. A single circuit can support up to 2400 watts in a track lighting system. *(Page 135)*

7. To provide good countertop lighting, you can install 20-watt fluorescent tubes or Little Inch fixtures beneath the upper cabinets to illuminate the countertops below. *(Pages 133 and 135)*

8. Low-voltage switching allows you to control many lights from a single switch panel, and it saves on the cost by using light gauge wire. *(Page 136)*

9. If a kitchen has more than one entrance, you should always install three- or four-way switches. This way, the homeowners can turn the lights on or off from any of the doors. The convenience of these switches is worth the small additional cost. *(Page 136)*

10. Most codes require you to install a GFCI on any switch or outlet that's within 4 feet of a sink. *(Page 136)*

Answers for Chapter 14

1. If you're in doubt that the floor is strong enough to support the brick veneer you'll install, have it analyzed by a licensed engineer before going ahead. *(Page 140)*

2. When using a plywood panel to distribute the weight of brickwork you'll install, cut it down so it's 1/2-inch less all around than the overall size of the brickwork. Then fill in the space with mortar after the brick is laid. *(Page 140)*

3. Cored brick is lighter in weight than solid brick, and it allows you to make your brickwork more stable by filling the holes with mortar during installation. *(Page 140)*

4. The standard formula for mortar used for laying brick is 1 part portland cement, 1 part hydrated lime and 6 parts sand. *(Page 141)*

5. To seal brick, use Thompson's Thoroseal or Prosoco's SureKlean. Both are effective. *(Page 142)*

6. To make a freestanding brick wall more stable, you would install headers every fifth course. *(Page 142)*

7. There are two advantages of a cavity brick wall over a solid one: First, the space between the bricks provides insulation; second, the space catches, collects and drains via weepholes any water that may penetrate the outer wall, preventing water from leaking into the building. *(Page 142)*

8. To secure a 4-inch brick wall to an existing wall, use corrugated metal wall ties, applied on top of every fifth course. Secure them with zinc-coated nails. *(Page 142)*

9. When you face a wall with split instead of whole brick, you save floor space, weight and money. *(Page 143)*

10. Corbeling the brick arch in Figure 14-9 allowed room to install extra counter space and drawers. *(Pages 143 and 145)*

Answers for Chapter 15

1. To start your own business, the first and most important qualification is confidence in yourself and in your ability as a kitchen designer. *(Page 149)*

2. The rule of thumb is that you should have six months of living expenses as a cushion when starting your business. *(Page 149)*

3. Even if you're working from your home, you need a separate phone line for your business. *(Page 149)*

4. When naming your business, choose a name that's easy to remember and readily associated with your business. It also helps if it's near the beginning of the alphabet so your yellow pages listing is near the top. *(Page 150)*

5. To be able to show your clients model kitchens and appliances, register with manufacturers' design showrooms in your area. *(Page 150)*

6. Your first step in finding customers is to take an ad in the yellow pages of your local phone directory. That's the most cost-effective place to advertise. *(Page 150)*

7. You should send a letter to general contractors every few months to remind them of your services. When they need kitchen design services, especially in a spec home, you want your name to come to mind. *(Pages 150-151)*

8. To help your showroom attract clients, first locate it in a busy area and use eye-catching signs. Then make the interior neat and well-lighted. Arrange your layout tastefully, adding color and contrast in the cabinet displays. *(Page 151)*

9. There are two important things to look for in hiring a salesperson — personality and expertise. But avoid applicants with a too-forceful personality. They are likely to antagonize the type of client you need most. *(Page 152)*

10. To determine applicants' design expertise, you could devise a test. Give them a standard kitchen plan and ask how they could improve on it. *(Page 153)*

Index

Other Practical References

Audiotapes: Estimating Remodeling Work

Listen to the "hands-on" estimating instructions in this popular remodeling seminar. Make your own unit price estimate based on the prints enclosed. Then check your completed estimate with those prepared in the actual seminar. After listening to these tapes you will know how to establish an operating budget for your business, determine indirect costs and profit, and estimate remodeling with the unit cost method.
Includes seminar workbook, project survey and unit price estimating form, and six 20-minute cassettes, $65.00

Basic Engineering for Builders

If you've ever been stumped by an engineering problem on the job, yet wanted to avoid the expense of hiring a qualified engineer, you should have this book. Here you'll find engineering principles explained in non-technical language and practical methods for applying them on the job. With the help of this book you'll be able to understand engineering functions in the plans and how to meet the requirements, how to get permits issued without the help of an engineer, and anticipate requirements for concrete, steel, wood and masonry. See why you sometimes have to hire an engineer and what you can undertake yourself: surveying, concrete, lumber loads and stresses, steel, masonry, plumbing, and HVAC systems. This book is designed to help the builder save money by understanding engineering principles that you can incorporate into the jobs you bid.
400 pages, 8½ x 11, $34.00

Builder's Guide to Accounting Revised

Step-by-step, easy-to-follow guidelines for setting up and maintaining records for your building business. A practical, newly-revised guide to all accounting methods showing how to meet state and federal accounting requirements and the new depreciation rules. Explains what the 1986 Tax Reform Act can mean to your business. Full of charts, diagrams, blank forms, simple directions and examples. **304 pages, 8½ x 11, $22.50**

Carpentry Estimating

Simple, clear instructions on how to take off quantities and figure costs for all rough and finish carpentry. Shows how to convert piece prices to MBF prices or linear foot prices, use the extensive manhour tables included to quickly estimate labor costs, and how much overhead and profit to add. All carpentry is covered; floor joists, exterior and interior walls and finishes, ceiling joists and rafters, stairs, trim, windows, doors, and much more. Includes *Carpenter's Dream* a material-estimating program, at no extra cost on a 5¼" high-density disk. Double-density 3½" or 5¼" disks are available for $10 extra. **336 pages, 8½ x 11, $35.50**

National Construction Estimator

Current building costs for residential, commercial, and industrial construction. Estimated prices for every common building material. Manhours, recommended crew, and labor cost for installation. Includes an electronic version of the book on computer disk with a stand-alone *Windows* estimating program **FREE** on a 3½" high-density (1.44 Mb) disk. If you need 5¼" high-density or 3½" double-density disks add $10 extra.
592 pages, 8½ x 11, $37.50. Revised annually

Contractor's Guide to the Building Code Revised

This completely revised edition explains in plain English exactly what the Uniform Building Code requires. Based on the most recent code, it covers many changes made since then. Also covers the Uniform Mechanical Code and the Uniform Plumbing Code. Shows how to design and construct residential and light commercial buildings that'll pass inspection the first time. Suggests how to work with an inspector to minimize construction costs, what common building shortcuts are likely to be cited, and where exceptions are granted. **544 pages, 5½ x 8½, $28.00**

Construction Forms & Contracts

125 forms you can copy and use — or load into your computer (from the FREE disk enclosed). Then you can customize the forms to fit your company, fill them out, and print. Loads into Word for Windows, Lotus 1-2-3, WordPerfect, or Excel programs. You'll find forms covering accounting, estimating, fieldwork, contracts, and general office. Each form comes with complete instructions on when to use it and how to fill it out. These forms were designed, tested and used by contractors, and will help keep your business organized, profitable and out of legal, accounting and collection troubles. Includes a 3½" high-density disk for your PC. For 3½" double-density, 5¼" high-density, or Macintosh disks, add $15.
432 pages, 8½ x 11, $39.75

Construction Surveying & Layout

A practical guide to simplified construction surveying. How to divide land, use a transit and tape to find a known point, draw an accurate survey map from your field notes, use topographic surveys, and the right way to level and set grade. You'll learn how to make a survey for any residential or commercial lot, driveway, road, or bridge — including how to figure cuts and fills and calculate excavation quantities. Use this guide to make your own surveys, or just read and verify the accuracy of surveys made by others.
256 pages, 5½ x 8½, $19.25

Concrete Construction & Estimating

Explains how to estimate the quantity of labor and materials needed, plan the job, erect fiberglass, steel, or prefabricated forms, install shores and scaffolding, handle the concrete into place, set joints, finish and cure the concrete. Full of practical reference data, cost estimates, and examples.
571 pages, 5½ x 8½, $20.50

Contractor's Survival Manual

How to survive hard times and succeed during the up cycles. Shows what to do when the bills can't be paid, finding money and buying time, transferring debt, and all the alternatives to bankruptcy. Explains how to build profits, avoid problems in zoning and permits, taxes, time-keeping, and payroll. Unconventional advice on how to invest in inflation, get high appraisals, trade and postpone income, and stay hip-deep in profitable work.
160 pages, 8½ x 11, $16.75

Construction Estimating Reference Data

Provides the 300 most useful manhour tables for practically every item of construction. Labor requirements are listed for sitework, concrete work, masonry, steel, carpentry, thermal and moisture protection, door and windows, finishes, mechanical and electrical. Each section details the work being estimated and gives appropriate crew size and equipment needed. This new edition contains *DataEst,* a computer estimating program on a high-density disk. This fast, powerful program and complete instructions are yours free on a high-density 5¼" disk when you buy the book. Double-density 5¼" or 3½" disks are available for $10 extra. **432 pages, 11 x 8½, $39.50**

Residential Electrical Estimating

A fast, accurate pricing system proven on over 1000 residential jobs. Using the manhours provided, combined with material prices from your wholesaler, you quickly work up estimates based on degree of difficulty. These manhours come from a working electrical contractor's records -- not some pricing agency. You'll find prices for every type of electrical job you're likely to estimate -- from service entrances to ceiling fans.
320 pages, 8½ x 11, $29.00

Drafting House Plans

Here you'll find step-by-step instructions for drawing a complete set of home plans for a one-story house, an addition to an existing house, or a remodeling project. This book shows how to visualize spatial relationships, use architectural scales and symbols, sketch preliminary drawings, develop detailed floor plans and exterior elevations, and prepare a final plot plan. It even includes code-approved joist and rafter spans and how to make sure that drawings meet code requirements. **192 pages, 8½" x 11, $27.50**

Estimating Electrical Construction

Like taking a class in how to estimate materials and labor for residential and commercial electrical construction. Written by an A.S.P.E. National Estimator of the Year, it teaches you how to use labor units, the plan take-off, and the bid summary to make an accurate estimate, how to deal with suppliers, use pricing sheets, and modify labor units. Provides extensive labor unit tables and blank forms for your next electrical job. **272 pages, 8½ x 11, $19.00**

Paint Contractor's Manual

How to start and run a profitable paint contracting company: getting set up and organized to handle volume work, avoiding mistakes, squeezing top production from your crews and the most value from your advertising dollar. Shows how to estimate all prep and painting. Loaded with manhour estimates, sample forms, contracts, charts, tables and examples you can use. **224 pages, 8½ x 11, $24.00**

Estimating Tables for Home Building

Produce accurate estimates for nearly any residence in just minutes. This handy manual has tables you need to find the quantity of materials and labor for most residential construction. Includes overhead and profit, how to develop unit costs for labor and materials, and how to be sure you've considered every cost in the job. **336 pages, 8½ x 11, $21.50**

Handbook of Construction Contracting

Volume 1: Everything you need to know to start and run your construction business; the pros and cons of each type of contracting, the records you'll need to keep, and how to read and understand house plans and specs so you find any problems before the actual work begins. All aspects of construction are covered in detail, including all-weather wood foundations, practical math for the job site, and elementary surveying. **416 pages, 8½ x 11, $24.75**

Volume 2: Everything you need to know to keep your construction business profitable; different methods of estimating, keeping and controlling costs, estimating excavation, concrete, masonry, rough carpentry, roof covering, insulation, doors and windows, exterior finishes, specialty finishes, scheduling work flow, managing workers, advertising and sales, spec building and land development, and selecting the best legal structure for your business. **320 pages, 8½ x 11, $26.75**

Manual of Professional Remodeling

The practical manual of professional remodeling that shows how to evaluate a job so you avoid 30-minute jobs that take all day, what to fix and what to leave alone, and what to watch for in dealing with subcontractors. Includes how to calculate space requirements; repair structural defects; remodel kitchens, baths, walls, ceilings, doors, windows, floors and roofs; install fireplaces and chimneys (including built-ins), skylights, and exterior siding. Includes blank forms, checklists, sample contracts, and proposals you can copy and use. **400 pages, 8½ x 11, $23.75**

National Building Cost Manual

Square foot costs for residential, commercial, industrial, and farm buildings. Quickly work up a reliable budget estimate based on actual materials and design features, area, shape, wall height, number of floors, and support requirements. Includes all the important variables that can make any building unique from a cost standpoint.
240 pages, 8½ x 11, $23.00. Revised annually

Profits in Building Spec Homes

If you've ever wanted to make big profits in building spec homes yet were held back by the risks involved, you should have this book. Here you'll learn how to do a market study and feasibility analysis to make sure your finished home will sell quickly, and for a good profit. You'll find tips that can save you thousands in negotiating for land, learn how to impress bankers and get the financing package you want, how to nail down cost estimating, schedule realistically, work effectively yet harmoniously with subcontractors so they'll come back for your next home, and finally, what to look for in the agent you choose to sell your finished home. Includes forms, checklists, worksheets, and step-by-step instructions. **208 pages, 8½ x 11, $27.25**

Estimating & Bidding for Builders & Remodelers w/ CD-ROM

If your computer has a CD-ROM drive, the CD Estimator disk enclosed in the book *Estimating & Bidding for Builders & Remodelers* could change forever the way you estimate construction. You get over 2,000 pages from five 1995 cost databases published by Craftsman, plus an estimating program you can master in minutes, plus a 40-minute interactive video on how to use this program, plus an award-winning book. This package is your best bargain for estimating and bidding construction costs.
272 pages, 8½ x 11, $69.50

Estimating Painting Costs

Here's an accurate step-by-step estimating system, based on easy-to-use manhour tables, for estimating painting costs from simple residential repaints to complicated commercial jobs — even heavy industrial and government work. Explains taking field measurements, doing take-offs from plans and specs, predicting productivity, figuring labor and material costs, and overhead and profit. Includes manhour and material tables, plus sample forms and checklists. **448 pages, 8½ x 11, $28.00**

Profits in Buying & Renovating Homes

Step-by-step instructions for selecting, repairing, improving, and selling highly profitable "fixer-uppers." Shows which price ranges offer the highest profit-to-investment ratios, which neighborhoods offer the best return, practical directions for repairs, and tips on dealing with buyers, sellers, and real estate agents. Shows you how to determine your profit before you buy, what "bargains" to avoid, and how to make simple, profitable, inexpensive upgrades. **304 pages, 8½ x 11, $19.75**

Remodeling Contractor's Handbook

Everything you need to know to make a remodeling business grow: identifying a market, inexpensive sales and advertising techniques that work, making accurate estimates, building a positive company image, training effective sales people, placing loans for customers, and bringing in profitable work to keep your company growing. **304 pages, 8½ x 11, $18.25**

Finish Carpenter's Manual

Everything you need to know to be a finish carpenter: assessing a job before you begin, and tricks of the trade from a master finish carpenter. Easy-to-follow instructions for installing doors and windows, ceiling treatments (including fancy beams, corbels, cornices and moldings), wall treatments (including wainscoting and sheet paneling), and the finishing touches of chair, picture, and plate rails. Specialized interior work includes cabinetry and built-ins, stair finish work, and closets. Also covers exterior trims and porches. Includes manhour tables for finish work, and hundreds of illustrations and photos. **208 pages, 8½ x 11, $22.50**

Roof Framing

Shows how to frame any type of roof in common use today, even if you've never framed a roof before. Includes using a pocket calculator to figure any common, hip, valley, or jack rafter length in seconds. Over 400 illustrations cover every measurement and every cut on each type of roof: gable, hip, Dutch, Tudor, gambrel, shed, gazebo, and more.
480 pages, 5½ x 8½, $22.00

Spec Builder's Guide

Shows how to plan and build a home, control construction costs, and sell to get a decent return on the time and money you've invested. Includes professional tips to ensure success as a spec builder: how government statistics help you judge the housing market, cutting costs at every opportunity without sacrificing quality, and taking advantage of construction cycles. Includes checklists, diagrams, charts, figures, and estimating tables. **448 pages, 8½ x 11, $27.00**

Wood-Frame House Construction

Step-by-step construction details, from the layout of the outer walls, excavation and formwork, to finish carpentry and painting. Contains all new, clear illustrations and explanations updated for construction in the '90s. Everything you need to know about framing, roofing, siding, interior finishings, floor covering and stairs — your complete book of wood-frame homebuilding. **320 pages, 8½ x 11, $19.75. Revised edition**

Running Your Remodeling Business

All about operating a remodeling business, from making your first sale to ensuring your profits: how to advertise, write up a contract, estimate, schedule your jobs, arrange financing (for both you and your customers), and when and how to expand your business. Explains insurance, bonds, and liens, and how to collect the money you've earned. Includes sample business forms. **272 pages, 8½ x 11, $21.00**

Stair Builders Handbook

If you know the floor-to-floor rise, this handbook gives you everything else: number and dimension of treads and risers, total run, correct well hole opening, angle of incline, and quantity of materials and settings for your framing square for over 3,500 code-approved rise and run combinations — several for every 1/8-inch interval from a 3 foot to a 12 foot floor-to-floor rise. **416 pages, 5½ x 8½, $15.50**

Rough Framing Carpentry

If you'd like to make good money working outdoors as a framer, this is the book for you. Here you'll find shortcuts to laying out studs; speed cutting blocks, trimmers and plates by eye; quickly building and blocking rake walls; installing ceiling backing, ceiling joists, and truss joists; cutting and assembling hip trusses and California fills; arches and drop ceilings — all with production line procedures that save you time and help you make more money. Over 100 on-the-job photos of how to do it right and what can go wrong. **304 pages, 8½ x 11, $26.50**

Roofing Construction & Estimating

Installation, repair and estimating for nearly every type of roof covering available today in residential and commercial structures: asphalt shingles, roll roofing, wood shingles and shakes, clay tile, slate, metal, built-up, and elastomeric. Covers sheathing and underlayment techniques, as well as secrets for installing leakproof valleys. Many estimating tips help you minimize waste, as well as insure a profit on every job. Troubleshooting techniques help you identify the true source of most leaks. Over 300 large, clear illustrations help you find the answer to just about all your roofing questions. **432 pages, 8½ x 11 x 11, $35.00**
